THE LIGHT WITHIN US

SHARON SALA

THE LIGHT WITHIN US

Acknowledgements:
Photo: Erin Kanske, Artsy Phartsy Photography
Formatting: Pam McCutcheon/Parker Hayden Media
Cover Design: The KILLION Group, Inc.

INTRODUCTION

This book is a compilation of my writings on my daily blog on social media. The works are pieces of me and messages received from spirit that I am led to pass on.

My path in this lifetime is to be a messenger. Through my works of both fiction and non-fiction, there is a continuing thread of joy, a search for a better way, and love conquering fear, darkness, and danger. Just as in the lives we live.

The message is simple... There is light within all of us, and the brighter our lights become, the farther away we move from bad decisions and life-changing choices.

And so it is.

§&

The city does not need the sun or the moon to shine upon it, for the glory of God gives it light, and the Lamb is its lamp. The nations will walk by light, and the kings of the earth will bring their splendor into it. —**Revelations 21:23-24**

We are souls born of light, and for the time we are living in human form, our paths are myriad, some crossing others along their way.

But the one thing we all strive for as we work to fulfill our soul contracts is to grow the light within us so that darkness of the soul is kept at bay.

Where there is nothing but light, darkness does not exist.

A NOTE FROM THE AUTHOR

I've posted stories and messages from Spirit on Facebook for years, and I also include names in my posts without identifying them. My Facebook friends and readers know who they are, but I'm posting a legend of sorts below, so you will also know of whom I speak.

My Mother passed during the writing of this last book. She was 98 and had been suffering from dementia for over 14 years, but when she forgot who I was, and then forgot herself, I began calling her Little Mama. Her passing was God's blessing, releasing her from years of a most terrible disease.

My Daddy was a special man to me. Both of his grandmothers were of The People. One was Cherokee. The other was Cree. He battled alcoholism during my childhood, but was twenty years sober when he passed. I loved him so much.

Grand and Grampy are my maternal grandparents and were the pivotal and guiding lights of my life when I was growing up.

Chris and Kathy are my children. Crissy is my niece, who I helped raise after my sister, Diane died.

Diane was my only sister and the only other sibling I had who lived past the day of their birth. She died two months after our Daddy's passing.

Scout is the name I use for my only grandson. He belongs to Kathy.

Ash, mentioned often in the posts, is Kathy's partner in life.

Chelsea, Logan, and Leslie are my Son's children.

Destiny, Devyn, and Courtney are Crissy's girls.

Denise cleans my house, but she's part of our family now.

I had a childhood sweetheart, who I found again after my second divorce. His name was Bobby. He was also of The People, from the Muscokee tribe, and was the love of my life. We had eight blessed years together before he died in my arms of cancer. I thought I might die with him, but it was not to be. My work here is not over. Bobby is with me in spirit, always. I can't see or hear him, but I feel him. As an Empath, dreaming and knowing are parts of my gift. He was my touchstone in life, and he is my guiding light now.

These people are my tribe.

The posts you are about to read are from Spirit, and from my heart, and I happily share them with you.

POINTS OF LIGHT

I was up early with the doves.

They sang to me from the treetops while I was watering plants in the back yard. Got that job done before the heat amped back up to the high 90s.

Bobby used to call me his Little Dove, but he said it in the Muscokee language. I can't remember what it was, and couldn't pronounce it when he said it, but I remember the gentleness in his voice, and the hug that came with it.

So I consider the dove song, my love song from him.

Your strength is greatest when it is not expounded in anger. When that happens, you have given away your light and energy to those who angered you.

Shouting won't change anything.

Neither will arguing.

If you need to be heard, bombard your enemy with phone calls and letters.

The written word goes farther, faster, than the curse that blew away with the wind.

Fifty-one years ago today, I was eleven days from giving birth to my second child (Kathy). I'm big as a barrel, aching in every joint, and standing in the kitchen freezing sweet corn. I had two bushel baskets of shucked corn in the floor yet to work up, and was working on blanching, cooling, and cutting corn off the cob to freeze when I heard the most ear-splitting shriek that had ever come out of my little boy's mouth. All I knew was that Chris, who was 2 1/2 years old, was outside playing only five minutes ago when I looked, and now this.

I dropped everything and ran, as scared as I've ever been in my life, that whatever was happening to him, I wouldn't be fast enough to save him.

I hit the storm door with the flat of my hand as I ran out onto the porch. Keep in mind, my baby is still screaming and I'm shouting, "I'm coming, baby.... Mama's coming."

I come out in the yard and I can't see him. Anywhere. But I can still hear the screams, and then I look into the old detached garage, which was where I parked the car, and there he was! Wedged under an old door that had been leaned up against the interior wall. But he wasn't stuck. He was just standing there, frozen...and screaming.

And just as I was running toward the garage, Mother came driving up from Seminole to help me freeze corn. She saw me running, and slammed her car into park and was out and following me, screaming, "what's wrong? what's wrong?"

But I didn't answer, because I didn't know. I just kept running.

The moment I got to him, I shoved that door a good three feet, before it fell over. That's when I saw the wasp nest. Red wasps...and the five wasps still on his little back, stinging him.

There are no words for the horror I felt, because he'd never been stung before, and I had no idea if he was allergic or not. If he was...and us five miles from a hospital, he'd could die before I'd get there with him.

I slapped the wasps away, and then realized there were even more stings. I have him wrapped up in my arms...his screams have turned to sobs, and we're running out of the garage.

We jumped in mother's car and she drove us straight to the Prague

Hospital...right into the arms of the best doctor/healer I ever knew...Kirk Mosley.

"Is he allergic?" they were asking, as they tore him out of my arms.

"I don't know! This is the first time he's been stung, and I was afraid to try and doctor him at home without knowing."

"Smart Mama," Dr. Mosley said, and then they began monitoring his breathing, and his pulse rate, and whatever else they had to do to determine his status. And all the while, Chris is sobbing and pointing at me.

"You want Mama?" Dr. Mosley asked, and Chris nodded.

Kirk looked at me...all red in the face from the heat and stress, tears in my eyes and a wet belly on my dress from the corn I'd been cutting, and then he smiled. "I can see why. She looks like the best, prettiest Mama I ever saw. Come here, Mama, you sit here and hold Chris, while we finish up."

The moment I sat down on the examining table and picked him up, the sobs quieted down. I held him belly to belly, leaving his back free for them to work, with his little arms around my neck, his head beneath my chin. He was shaking so hard from the pain that when he talked, the words came out in fits and starts, like they were being jerked from his body.

"I'm so sorry, baby," I kept saying, and rocking him against me.

"Hurts, Mama," was all that he could say.

Mother is sitting in a chair watching both of us, blinking back tears. She's the stoic kind. The kind who weeps only from within.

The good news was that he wasn't allergic. The bad news was he had nine red wasp stingers in his back that they had to pull out. But Chris never cried from that again. He left the crying up to me.

We got home a couple of hours later. My husband was sitting in the living room with a scowl on his face when we walked in. I'm carrying Chris and Mother saw his scowl and frowned right back at him.

"Where have you been? You've got corn to put up," he said.

Before I could answer, Mother pointed out the front door.

"You have a nest of red wasps in the garage that you need to get rid of. This baby was stung nine times. If you were so worried about the corn, why weren't you in there cutting it off the cob? You know how."

And that was the end of that.

So today, I am remembering the quiet mother I knew, who never backed down from the bear between her and hers. Even if the bear was a cranky son-in-law.

He went out to do what he was told. Chris got a grape Popsicle, and Mother and I froze the corn. Forty pints of corn was frozen that day, and eleven days later, my baby girl was born.

Chris was not enamored. He took one look at her in my arms and told me to take her back.

&.

Daddy used to call me his little firecracker because I was born on the 3rd of July...only a short time before midnight of the 4th.

Only I wasn't a firecracker personality.

I was, and still am, quiet and observant.

I can remember sitting in my Grand's dining room in their old two-story farmhouse, plunking on the piano and imagining the music I was making was grand, and the songs I was singing were glorious.

All of the adults were in the front room, which is what the living room was called, because it was at the front of the house, and I heard Mother say..."that child is just like me. She can't carry a tune in a wooden bucket."

Some of the others laughed, but my Grand shushed them right up with a short admonition. "You hush up and let her be...she's making music."

And I was...just not the kind anyone might want to hear.

But even then, I had this constant urge to create...my hands were always busy...from sitting in the driveway out on the farm making mud pies, to making playhouses in the trees. Twisting, bending...patting, sticking....my fingers never stopped moving.

I drummed them on the table waiting for Mother to bring our supper plates to the table. I twisted the curls in my hair into tangles. I couldn't talk without my hands helping me tell a story.

When I learned to type in high school, I got really good at it, really fast. I could do sixty, and then eighty words a minute without blinking...and then even more. And when electric typewriters became available, my speed went straight up to one hundred and twenty words a minute.

As I grew older, sewing and cooking became my creative outlets, and then painting in oils and acrylics. I needed it. I needed this to make me feel fulfilled.

But I never could make the pictures I was painting on canvas, look quite like the picture I had in my head.

I always loved to read, but on the day I discovered writing, it was like a light turned on in my head.

THIS WAS IT!

This was what my fingers had been practicing for in typing class! This was what I was supposed to do with all my dreams.

And the pictures I learned to paint with words, were far better than the pictures I painted with oils and acrylics.

That was then...and this is now.

If you feel like you're on the verge of discovering your passion, but can't quite see it...just wait.

When it's time--When you're ready.

You will burst into bloom as the creator YOU came to be.

Whatever your medium, it will be the right one for you.

❧

Seeing faces of strangers and feeling either an instant connection, or immediate dislike is soul recognition.

It comes from an accumulation of lifetimes and the soul memory within us.

For the ones you sense immediate dislike, it can be a warning that they have betrayed you before, or you have hurt them in another lifetime, and that you have karma to work out.

The greatest gift to both of you would to somehow heal that old trauma. But your path and free will influence all of that.

Sometimes all it takes is to not engage in ill will this time around.

To be the peacemaker, not the warrior.

That's what soul work is about...working out the kinks of what went wrong in another life, and learning how to navigate through life-times of regret.

When that happens, everything within you changes...how you view life...how you find joy when all you could see before kept you down. That's how you grow your soul...how you grow your light.

Those are life lessons.

You will feel the change within you almost immediately.

Waking up without a sense of heaviness around you.

Going through your day without that chip on your shoulder.

Being able to see happiness for what it is...good health, safety, comfort, peace within your space, and love for humanity as a whole, not just your immediate circle.

Loving strangers isn't about the love between partners, or family. It's about wanting everyone to have what they need. Empathizing for tragedies without taking them as your burden to bear.

Giving of yourself to others without notice, or expectations.

Doing it because it's the right thing to do.

We didn't come here to accumulate anything but understanding and knowledge.

The old saying...'you can't take it with you' means more than you know.

It's true that all the power and wealth, or the acrimony and guilt...whichever it is you have made your world about in this life-time...does not go with you.

They will go back with knowledge. Knowledge that they focused on all the wrong things...that they made money their goal.

When those people transition back to the souls they were, they will both realize that they had the same faults...they chased the same prize...one succeeded...the other did not...but they were both focusing on the wrong thing.

What they do take back is a mistake that has to be rectified, which means....they'll be back, in another lifetime...with the goal of healing the karma they caused others.

That's called soul work, and we're either here to work, or here to teach.

꙾

Had an outdoor cover shoot this morning for my non-fiction book...the first one I'm self-pubbing from my FB posts...kind of an inspirational/humor genre. Kathy went with me. It was fun and it didn't take all that long. The downside was getting up before six a.m. to get to the location in Arcadia, and getting it over with before the day got too hot.

Can't wait to get it finished and uploaded. I'm already editing it during the day, and writing on my new Blessings book at night.

Wisdom is knowing when to STOP.

Patience comes when you have run out of bad things to say about whatever it was that delayed you.

Have you ever had a hissy fit and no one was around to see or hear you, for which you are grateful, because you feel like a dumb ass for acting that way?

I have.

I have worn myself out being angry at someone else, and the only one who suffered was me.

I don't do that anymore.

Wisdom is knowing when to STOP..

If you ever had a time in your life when there wasn't enough to eat, then your life turned around, and that poverty phase was gone, it's hard to get out of that way of thinking.

Like eating too much of what you have now because you remember not having enough.

Like hoarding food in every nook and cranny, because the part of you that suffered hunger and discomfort is telling your subconscious to stock up.

And then you learn to believe in yourself and your ability to always furnish what you need, and you learn how to STOP that destructive behavior.

It's all about trusting yourself.

Wisdom is accepting the human frailties for what they are.

Anger comes from fear.

Rage comes from a sense of danger. Fight or flight.

Lying is a way of skirting issues you don't want to talk about.

Cheating is the lazy way of getting what you want, irregardless of what it does to others.

Pride and Ego go hand in hand. Too much of either one is detrimental to your happiness.

Choosing to live as a victim is easier than overcoming what made you feel that way.

When you understand the human condition is to suffer, learn, and grow, then the easiest way to keep from becoming part of the problem, is just by walking away.

Often, the chaos around us has nothing to do with us personally.

When you have the wisdom to see where you stand within any given situation, then you can always find the door out of it.

It's like how you were taught to cross a street.

STOP LOOK LISTEN

And then proceed.

࿆

Busy day.

Finally got home and ate lunch after 1:00 p.m. and now I'm sleepy. LOL Like a baby...feed me and I'll go to sleep.

But not sleeping yet. I have work to do.

Great news from my oldest granddaughter last night. She is an event planner in Dallas, and she just landed a great new job with the company she's been wanting to work for. Proud of you, Chelsea!!

I dreamed all night...the first half of the night was about a frog painting. Every time I tried to claim it, the frog would change colors...from all shades of green, to red-rimmed eyes. I know frogs evolve from little wormy looking tadpoles to a whole other being, growing legs and feet, and an actual body. So, my dream was an analogy for growing and evolving from one thing to another, and yes, I'm doing that. We're all doing that as we no longer accept the status quo. We are growing a new generation that believes in advocating for all, not just the chosen few.

Coming home from errands I saw a three-car wreck, and about two blocks closer to home, a police car came flying up behind us all, lights flashing and siren screaming, and headed East toward Lake Thunderbird. All I could do was pray for those who were in need and stay out of the way. The energy was high and way out of balance. Glad to get home.

Yesterday was the anniversary of the day I lost Bobby. I knew it. I thought about it. I miss him. But I wasn't sad. It's taken me years to get to this place...and the fact that I know he never really left me helps, too. I can feel him with me, although I can't see him, and only rarely hear his voice as I'm going to sleep.

So I gave the day to him. I talked about him with friends. We laughed about his, 'star of the show', personality. I rejoiced for the years we had together without counting the ones since his passing. Where he is, time does not exist.

For him, it will only be a blink of the eye before I'm with him again.

I'm the one who's had to learn patience.

I know he laughs.

I don't like to wait.

On anybody.

But for him, I'll do whatever it takes.

§♠

Well...it's taken me about two weeks of just deleting post after post, but I almost have a friendly FB feed again.

Today is a voting day in my state, but I voted early last Saturday so I wouldn't have to stand in lines. <3

One Easter when my sister and I were about eleven and twelve, Mother and Daddy gave us two baby ducks. They were so cute, and fluffy and yellow and they moved in unison, like they were tied together at the wings or something, so we named them DuckDuck.

We played with DuckDuck all the time, until they were so bonded with us that they followed us all over the farm. If we were on foot, they were right behind us, talking, talking, talking, quack, quack, quack,

quack. Diane and I would quack back at them, which would send them into something of a frenzy.

About every other day, my sister and I had to go into the garden and pick tomatoes, or green beans, or dig some potatoes for dinner. It was always something. And DuckDuck went with us. They loved it when we were picking tomatoes and stayed right under our feet, fighting to see who got the next green horn worm that we'd pull off the tomato plants. The DuckDucks would go crazy, quacking with delight at the big fat worms they were getting.

When mid-summer came, the days were so long and hot, and we played in our water sprinkler in the front yard, with DuckDuck running through the water with us.

One day Daddy got the idea to take them to the pond and let them play down there, so we all started walking to the pond with DuckDuck right behind us...quack, quack, quack. But when we got there, they ignored the water and stood beside us. So Daddy picked one up and put him into the water at the very edge.

OMG! The quacking and feather beating, and water flying was everywhere, like DuckDuck was being murdered. He scrambled out of that water, quacking his dismay.

That's when it hit us. No one had taught them to swim. They didn't know they could!

So Diane and I took off our shoes and waded into the water, thinking they would follow. Instead, they stood on the pond bank and quacked frantically at us.

Poor little DuckDucks. They were afraid of water.

Then Daddy, being such a man of little patience, just picked them up and gave them a toss. Diane and I were screeching.."no, Daddy, no!" But they were already in the water.

There is no way to describe the flapping and squawking, and swimming that ensued. But they did swim...right out of the water, and took off toward the house by themselves, quacking in high dismay at what had happened.

Diane and I ran to catch up, then picked them up and carried them, stroking their long necks and slick feathers, and talking to them in soft, soothing voices, telling them we were sorry, and we wouldn't let that mean Daddy do that to them again. They tucked their heads up beneath our chins and murmured the softest little cluck/quacks to us, like they were telling us how awful it was, and how scared they were.

Our DuckDucks.

No one could have loved them more, but they didn't know the duck world. Only ours.

They were truly 'ducks out of water.'

We had them about two or three years, and eventually, they took themselves back to the pond and became very attached to it. It became their true home, and it was where they stayed until one morning they weren't there.

We never knew for sure what happened to them.

Daddy told us a coyote might have gotten them...or a snapping turtle.

But we wanted to believe they'd flown away.

DuckDuck came into our lives, and stayed until they had some-place else to be.

Like the people who are our friends for a while, and then we outgrow each other and move on--grateful to have known them, but knowing they weren't forever.

Like life. We live it and then we don't, but during the time we are together, we have shared laughter and sorrows, joys and pain. And we have come to a greater understanding of what it means to share time and space with someone you love.

I want to live my life to the max, and grow my soul light so bright that even after I'm gone, you will still be able to see the path I was on.

&.

More rain and thunderstorms last night. Came in here a little after 3:00 a.m. I got up to check the weather, then went back to bed. Nothing but some wind and a lot of rain, which is a blessing for us.

Denise is here cleaning, and she's a whirlwind.

I'm in the office staying out of her way. :)

omg...I just mixed up my Plexus protein shake for the day. I picked Chocolate this morning and I threw a handful of fresh pitted cherries into the blender before I made it. Cherry chocolate surprise. Yummmmy.

Since I'm unable to eat meat anymore, I'm always looking for healthy protein based foods, and this shake is the bomb for getting in my daily protein. As much as I like eggs and cheese for protein, I can get tired of them. And beans without meat to season them are blah. I use some Vegan flavoring products, but nothing on earth can successfully replace the flavor of smoked pork in a pot of beans, or bacon drippings cooked in with the black-eyed peas. That's how I was raised, so for my taste buds, that's how food is supposed to taste. LOLOL

So I manage. And today, I celebrate my cherry-chocolate shake.

Finished the first chapter of new Blessings book last night. Some books are slow to get into...even though I know the whole story before I write it. But this time it started with a bang. Makes writing so much easier not to be struggling on how to transition smoothly from one scene to the next.

Something to think about:

Every soul comes from ONE SOURCE, which means we're all connected to God. No matter what name you call Him, He is the ONLY SOURCE. Skin color is just the choice we made before we came. The region on Earth we chose to live in this life time is connected to the Purpose for why we're here. Free Will was given to all of us.

So while you're all busy using your Free Will to sort yourselves by skin color and religion, by beliefs and purposes, the bottom line is that we're all part of the great I Am.

And this sorting you're doing is just a fear-based way of stepping into human shoes. None of us come with the thought that this place is heaven on earth, and we love it so much that we don't ever want to leave. We're here to learn...to do soul work...

Some souls remember their purpose for coming, but most do not, and so the mere fact of navigating human existence is often frustrating and frightening. Thus the sorting and separating...

If only you could remember how many other lifetimes you've had, and how many times your skin was a different color from what it is right now, you would forget about being afraid of what you don't know, and concentrate on what you came here to do.

At that point, we would all be able to live in harmony and peace.

The first step out of fear is knowledge.

❧

Big thunderstorms last night...No tornado threats, just hard straight winds, rain and lightning. Power was out for several hours, but came back on just about daylight.

It's predicted to do it again today, and it looks like it will outside.

I just had my yard mowed yesterday and there are so many pine cones in the back yard now that blew off of the tree on the other side of my back fence. I'll be picking those up again, but I'm gonna wait until this next round passes.

I moved the bird feeder to the back porch last night before it began to rain. Didn't want l the seed to get wet and sprout like it's done before. So...this morning when I looked out, it was obvious the birds found it anyway...seed scattered all over the place and a couple of little bird calling cards (poop) for their trouble. hahaha

I dreamed hard all night until I woke up and found out the power was off. I was still halfway between the dream world and here, and there were rainbow colors on the ceiling of my bedroom, but the house felt wrong. I glanced at my cell phone for time. It was 4:44. Sometimes angels send us messages numerically..because mathematics/physics/binary code, etc...because math is the language of the Universe.

So, I looked up those numbers in my Angel Number book.

In the book the numbers 444 says, There are angels--they are everywhere around you! You are completely loved, supported, and guided by many Heavenly beings, and you have nothing to fear.

With those comforting words, I told myself it was just the energy of the storm that I was feeling, and I went back to bed without concern.

There were two odd moments in my dreams that I woke up with today.

One was a brief glimpse of an old woman wearing an orange leather jacket. She had the collar pulled up and was holding it across the bottom half of her face, as if to mask herself, but she looked straight at me as she moved from south to north across my line of vision.

And them the other odd moment was seeing a white, late model pickup flying past my line of vision again, and moving from north to south. So I woke up wondering if the old woman caught herself a ride to wherever she was going.

I have no idea what either of these meant, and wish that had been my Little Mama hitching a ride to heaven, but she wouldn't be caught dead in orange...and yes...that was a joke...my irony for the day.

⁊

Woke up to thunder and a nice shower. I won't have to water plants again today. Yay!!

I had such a great time at the Summer Solstice party last night.

Yummy food with good friends and quiet moments outside sitting around the fire pit, full of gratitude for new beginnings, and dodging a few June bugs that were dive-bombing the porch light behind us. :)

Be mindful of your words and thoughts.

They create the environment of your world.

The Law of Attraction states that what you give out into the world, you will get back.

Remember that when you are judging and making fun of other people, that you have just requested the same thing to happen to you.

Only you'll be mad when it happens, and wailing loud and long at how mean people are being to you. And you won't remember that you asked for it.

You won't remember that you were cautioned.

And then you were warned.

And you did it anyway because everyone laughed with you when you belittled someone else.

You won't remember, because you don't believe.

And that's okay, too.

It's your life. Your free will. Your choices to make.

I choose a peaceful life.

That's my free will.

And I do believe.

❦

Going to a summer solstice party tonight...celebrate the arrival of summer. May as well rejoice because it comes, whether you're ready for the heat or not.

However, it also signifies change and growth, and I'm all about moving forward, so I'm going to welcome it.

I dreamed all night. Like head-hopping from one movie to another without ever seeing the ending of any of them.

Those dreams are exhausting. I woke up early, rolled over and went back to sleep. That time I actually rested without dreaming.

I had my Plexus Slim, and my Plexus protein shake after I got up, and now I'm all about the day. :)

I began a new story. It's another one for the Blessings series. Tentative title is A Rainbow Above Us. All I will tell you now is that the hero's name is Bowie James. And there's an old, old feud in his family's past.

We've all heard or said "they crossed a line."

Like someone went too far beyond propriety...or a law.

But there's another way to look at that phrase if you give it a twist by saying, "those are the people who color outside the lines."

That's not a bad thing.

That just means they see another way of doing the same thing.

I'm one of those people who color outside the lines.

I always see life a little differently than the norm.

I remember once when I was small, living in an old house with a leaky roof. Every time it rained, Mother and Daddy were grabbing milk buckets, and water buckets and big cook pots to catch the drips...which were many.

Everyone was worried about the water coming into the house, and I was sitting down playing near the buckets, listening to the different sounds the drips made when they hit the water. I heard music. I imagined myself in a boat in a storm.

Once Mother dropped a whole pitcher of cream in the kitchen floor and cried, because cream was precious. She'd skimmed it off the milk to take to town to sell. I was so sorry Mother was crying, but then I saw a little brown bug on the floor that was running hell bent for leather trying to get away from the flood of cream, and it let it run onto my hand and carried it out to save it.

I lost track of the tragedy in my effort to save a bug.

Same world. Different eyes.

So for all the people like me, who color outside the lines, rejoice in being different.

When you stand out for being different, you'll never get lost in the crowd.

Your conscience is an echo, reminding you over and over and over that you will never be free of the guilt until you make amends.

The height of stupidity is doing the same thing over and over and over and expecting the end result to change.

Despite how you were raised, if you are an adult, you know by now there are other ways to react besides the fit you are having and the ass you are making of yourself.

Life is hard so that by the time we grow old, it makes leaving easier.

It's a simple fix to just say, I'm sorry, rather than talking for an hour trying to justify the mistake you just made.

Country sayings that make me laugh:

Your ass is grass.

(a reference that means, someone is likely to kill you for whatever you've done.)

The high center in them ruts is all the way up to your butt crack.

(a reference to how deep the ruts are in a muddy road)

Don't just stand there. Do somethin', even if it's wrong.

(a reference for a dislike to idle people)

He sold his good sense for a nickel and lost it down the drain.

(a reference to someone with no common sense)

Awww, HELL no! Here! Hold my beer!

(a reference to the fist fight that is about to begin)

She's skinnier than a starvin' pup. Somebody give her a biscuit.

(no explanation necessary)

This is a true description of the girl I was, and the woman I am.

I may wear earrings in my ears, and makeup on my face, but you can't hide the country in a girl who grew up with sand between her toes.

ཕ

Many years ago when I was still living on the farm with Mother and Daddy, but working in the city at Tinker Air Force Base, I missed my car pool ride, and had to drive myself to work.

Other than being a hassle, it was no big deal.

The sun was moments away from dawn, but it appeared it was going to be a gray, miserable kind of day. Like it might blow up a rain...or it might not.

I was about halfway between Prague and Harrah on Highway 62 and turning a curve when all of a sudden, I drove into a fog bank that was so thick I couldn't see the end of the car. I slammed on the brakes and steered toward what I thought the side of the road would be and stopped.

It threw me off balance so fast I didn't know what to do. I suddenly had no sense of up or down, or where I was. I was scared to death that I'd be hit by another car on that two-lane road, and rolled down the window to see if I could hear traffic coming, only to realize sound was so muffled within that cloud that when I shouted out the window, even my own voice was muted. Then to my horror, the fog began spilling into my car and I frantically rolled the window back up.

So there I sat, praying not to be hit by another car. Praying for the fog to pass. Praying for help.

A couple of minutes passed, with me becoming more and more panicked. What to do? What to do?

Have you ever been too scared to cry?

And then all of a sudden, this feeling moved through me, like wind through an open window, and without hearing a word, I knew I was no longer alone.

My heartbeat hit normal rhythm once more.

All the tension melted from my body.

And there I sat, in perfect calm.

I didn't hear anything, but the word Wait was in my head.

I couldn't see anything, but I felt the word Safe.

Within the space of about five minutes, the fog began to dissipate. And still I waited.

I could see the hood of my car, and the railing of the old bridge on the east side of Harrah, just as you're entering the town.

Then I could see the whole bridge...and then bits of early morning sunlight.

As the fog was fading away, I felt an absence of spirit and knew I was once again, by myself. But I also knew in that moment, that i was also, never alone.

I pulled back onto the highway and continued on to work, crying grateful tears.

That was the same feeling I had years later when my Daddy and my Sister died within two months of each other. Panic. I was lost. Untethered from the anchor of family.

It happened again losing Bobby.

And it happened again when I began losing Little Mama.

The only difference between that foggy morning and the panic in later years was that I'd learned what to do.

I Waited. And I Trusted, knowing answers would come.

When you feel like you are facing the world on your own,

I am here to testify that you are not.

All you have to do is ask for help.

Then wait.

And listen.

You may not hear the words aloud, but the answer will be given, and you will act, thinking you figured it out alone.

Only you didn't.

Your decision was the angel whisper in your ear.

The voice you call your conscience is your own soul, guiding the human part of you to safety.

Standing in the God-light of life is the surest path to any destination.

❧

We are being tested every waking moment of our lives.
Is that safe to eat?
What we tell our children.
Who we are willing to trust.
Who we choose to work for.
How fast we choose to drive, regardless of a speed limit.
Do you give back money you see someone drop?
Do you find money and turn it in or keep it?
Do you cheat on a test?
Do you cheat on a partner?
Do you put your family at risk just to satisfy your desires?
Looking away because it's easier than facing a hard truth?
All these and thousands more- every day.
We were given free will before we came here.
And the choices we make from that result in consequences.
With each consequence comes a lesson.
Our purpose is to learn from it. Not repeat it.
When we are tested, we're not learning from a book.
We are learning about life.
How many times do you want to take the same test?
How many lifetimes will it take you to learn a simple kindness works miracles, instead of the damage you cause from hate?
The choice is yours to make.

❧

Wonderful message at Love Church about being authentic. Being who God made you to be. No matter what anyone else thinks about you or your lifestyle, or how you dress, or the work you do, has NO bearing on you. God doesn't make mistakes.

So, yes, today is Father's Day,.

I'd say the posts are about half and half as to praising a good father, or angry about a bad one.

Good fathers can have bad children.

And good children can have bad fathers, or no present father at all,.

So here's the deal, people.

If you had a bad father, that's on him, not you.

Don't own HIS mistakes by keeping him alive in your world with bad memories and old pain. Don't bring him up every father's day just to remind yourself that you were a victim then.

You're not a victim now. You either escaped it, or lived through it.

Either way, you are a survivor.

Survivors are strong people.

They experienced trauma and survived.

This day is just a day for remembrance and nothing else.

If the memory isn't worth keeping, then let it be.

I AM OPEN AND RECEPTIVE TO ALL GOOD.

❧

What a day. I could have slept in, but I was awake at 8:00 a.m., so I got up.

Started laundry and checked email because I have a new project in the works. New books from my FB posts. It took me days to separate them into the subject matter, but I'm good to go on the first one. Sending the posts off to be scanned and formatted into a Word file then edits, then back to have edits formatted for ebook and print.

I did Laundry this morning.

Got oil changed and got a free car wash out of the deal.

Had a single dip of vanilla frozen custard from Rusty's Custard Factory, here on East Main. Best frozen custard ever.

And I'm home.

I didn't talk to a soul until sometime around 1:00 p.m. today.

Yesterday was pretty much the same way.

A good time to withdraw and reflect.

When you don't know the difference between a truth and a lie, then why are you spreading the story?

Some people communicate with conflict, because it's the only way they know how to be heard. Even though I understand how they got that way...usually what they witnessed growing up...surely as an adult, you see the futility of trying to make a point by screaming curse words in someone else's face.

Once you've hurt someone you know, someone you liked or loved, and said hurtful, unforgivable things to them, they can never be unheard, and saying "I'm sorry" doesn't make it go away.

Ever.

Just because it was done to you, doesn't mean you should pass on the pain.

৯৯

So Daddy, another Father's Day, and here we are again.

33 years since you've been gone.

I've already outlived you by 10 years and you are just as real and alive to me now as when you were still here.

All I have to do is smell Old Spice aftershave, or the aroma of a pipe full of Prince Albert tobacco...or hear a song or someone whistling, and you are right there with me....and I know it.

I don't cry because you're not here. I celebrate the years you were.

I honor the man you wanted to be...the one you meant to be, when alcohol didn't cloud things up. I put all the sad stuff and the bad stuff away years ago. It belongs to the me I was, and the you you were before you kicked it's ass. Twenty years sober. So I had the best of you when I was little, and I had the best of you after I was grown. Can't ask for anything more.

You taught me how to fish, and then how to clean them.

You taught me how to drive in a hay meadow, and how to change flats. You wanted to make sure that I could take care of myself when you weren't around.

At 6'4", you were a giant to me when I was little. As a child, my first view of the world was from your shoulders. Strong as an ox, tender-hearted to a fault.

I still hear you and your brothers laughing at the Smith family gathering. I could pick your laugh out from all of them.

You served your country. You cherished your family. You rose above your weakness like the warrior I always knew you to be.

Your Cherokee grandmother is proud of you.

Your Cree grandmother is proud of you.

In my mind I see you with all of your family, still telling jokes and laughing...riding that big paint horse, your black hair shining in the sunlight and that big smile on your face.

I picture you and Ruth sitting on the banks of some pond, or out in a boat on a lake, fishing, with a dog sleeping in the shade nearby.

Thank you for being my Daddy.

In the end, you were everything I needed you to be.

Love you.

Miss you.

Save me a seat beside you at the pond.

I still love to fish.

Controversy, Fear, Anger, Grief.

These negative emotions are swamping the planet (not just here). And it's all part of the growing division between 3D and 5D. I said it the other day, and I'll say it again.

There is no more in-between for good and bad.

There aren't any more fences to ride.

And the media feeds all of the controversy, fear, anger, and grief to us, face-slap after face-slap, so that when one scandal begins to fade, they have more to keep people angry or afraid.

ANGER AND FEAR FEED NEGATIVITY.

And everything negative keeps the puppets jumping, which is the goal of behind the scene power brokers..

A good portion of our country buys into everything the media says, because it used to be a reliable source of news.

Newspapers, then television news, WERE the in-between.

They WERE the ones who verified facts before anything was broadcast or went into print.

But when "in-between" disappeared within the Shift, they chose a side.

The reason I'm pointing all of this out is to give you pause...to be able to step back, see the logic of what's happening to ALL OF US, and how we're being manipulated.

They don't want us to find ways to get along.

When the Whole is of one mindset...a mindset of peace for all with the freedom to know different is the way it's supposed to be, then the Whole cannot be divided.

And if there is no way to divide a nation,

Then there is no way to control it.

Don't buy into the bullshit.

It can't be substantiated.

And it washes away when it rains.

&

Social Media is like the family at Grandma's house right after Sunday Dinner. Everyone is full, and gossip is being shared, and everyone there has an opinion of how they should have handled their trauma drama.

It may feel intrusive to some, and it's often unwelcome, unasked for advice, but the bottom line is...at least this was true in my Grandma's house...it was all given with love and a true appreciation to want to help.

You can all do what I do...let them talk and then do it my way. LOL

AND I'M ADDING AN ADDENDUM BECAUSE I WASN'T CLEAR ENOUGH WITH MY PURPOSE.

My post about FB is not Criticism. It's not a complaint. It's an Observation..

When I was a little girl, our only piece of technology was a battery powered radio, because at that time electricity had not come to rural

Oklahoma.

Mother listened to a soap opera called Stella Dallas in the afternoon when Diane and I were supposed to be taking a nap. Sometimes she'd be shelling peas, or breaking beans, but always working...

She also listened to a program that was all hit songs of the day, and this morning as I was working around the house, part of a verse from one of the songs popped into my head..."how high the moon", and for an instant, I was back in that time, listening to Nat King Cole.

"Somewhere there's music,

How faint the tune.

Somewhere there's heaven.

How high the Moon."

It was a lullaby for our nap time.

Not an easier, better time in our world....but a gentler time.

Bad behavior, is bad behavior.

Using the excuse, "it's how I was raised," only points a finger at your parents for their lack, and a finger at you for knowing there's a kinder way and still not doing it.

❧

Today was 'be kind to Sharon' day.

I took her to get a massage and then a session of reflexology.

She said, "thank you, very much."

I said, "But of course, my friend. After all, you do so much for me."

The sands of time run through an old hourglass.

The hands of time spin around a twelve-hour clock.

Time is measured by birthdays.

By how long it's been since a loved one passed.

By how long it's going to take for a steak to cook medium well.

By how how long I have to write a book vs the looming deadline.

By the precious few extra minutes you get to sleep late on a snow day.

Before it mattered...time was only daylight and dark.

Living life by a clock is the fastest way to burnout.

Find something you love, and do it.

Don't say you don't have time, because you do. Somewhere in the hectic life you have created for yourself, there will be time for you.

But you have to find it, then choose it.

There will come a time in your life when you will be glad you did.

֍

People go through times of plenty, and times of scarcity.

They will experience good health, and then have a period of time when it seems as if they can't get ahead of one injury or illness before another pops up.

They will have periods of great joy and then tragedy will strike, and the anchor of certainty is yanked out from under them.

God isn't 'giving' you the good times, nor is He responsible for the bad. Those things are what your life is comprised of, this time around.

None of it has to do with being punished, and none of it has to do with being rewarded. It is just life--plain and simple.

Your job, at all times, is negotiating your way through it.

You are not supposed to throw up your hands and look around for someone to rescue you just because you have troubles.

The lesson is to find your way through it, and if one thing doesn't work, that's just Plan A. You simply go to Plan B.

You say you didn't have a Plan B?

Well, you do now, because A didn't work.

That's how you evolve...by growth and understanding of the human condition.

The only thing you really have to remember is:

Don't quit.

Don't say, I can't.

Say, I will.

In all things...it is the power of positive thinking that moves you toward the optimum destination.

It may not be the destination you were expecting, but it is where life took you, so if you're there, then it's where you were meant to be.

֍

The summer of my discontent.

It began with the permanent my mother gave me. My hair was curly. A little wayward, especially on windy days, which in Oklahoma language means always. Mother did not abide wayward or untidy.

Someone told her a permanent was a good way to control curly hair. You know...rolling it on those tiny little plastic rods(came in one size only back then) so tight it gave you a temporary brow lift. Mother liked neat and tight. Until she took them out. She was irked that it hadn't worked. She wasn't looking at what she'd done from my point of view. I bawled.

My hair looked like a dandelion looks at the point of getting ready to shed its seeds. Fuzz wuz the word. I bawled again. She took me to have it cut. All it did was leave me with short fuzz. At that point, she was done and the rest was left up to me...which meant stop bawling, and live with it until it grew out.

That was all well and good, except that was also the year I decided boys weren't obnoxious pests, anymore. They had become an interesting species. One that I wanted to explore.

Maybe this was the Universe's way of protecting me from myself that summer. I mean...I didn't have much sense...but my appearance became the armor my mother would have wanted me in, to protect me from 'those boys".

So I moped, read books, ran through the pasture with my sister, and down to the draw where the sand plums grew, then stood beneath the sparse shade and ate semi-green plums that gave us a belly-ache, and dreamed of marrying Elvis.

For my eleventh birthday, Mother and Daddy gave me a little record player. I bought my first 45, (that's rpm, not caliber). It was Elvis Presley's, Love Me Tender, and on the flip side was You Ain't Nothin' But a Hound Dog.

Revenge was sweet. I played that same song over and over all summer, as loud as the audio would go on that record player. Daddy was either cursing or laughing about it, and Mother was stoically silent. She'd already fried my hair.

She didn't have it in her to fry my dreams of marrying, Elvis, too.

My hair grew out. She trimmed off the fried ends again. School began, and so did the first county 4-H meeting of the year in Okemah. We were at the hall, circling up to do the Hokey Pokey. I looked up, then saw a boy watching me from across the room. He grinned. I blushed and looked down at my feet.

More shuffling was still going on as everyone was getting into the big circle...and someone slipped between me and the boy on my left. I looked up again. It was him. Black hair, dark eyes twinkling, prettiest brown skin, and oh so cute.

"Hi. I'm Bobby. What's your name?"

"Sharon."

And then the song began to play. "You put your left foot in. You put your left foot out....

Elvis had just lost his place in line.

ॐ

Kathy and Ash are here making a pretty border around the Bradford Pear tree in my front yard. They dug the Bermuda grass out from around it in about a four foot circle, put down rock, and then bordered it with gray bricks. It looks so nice. Now when I water it, the water will go to the roots.

I made potato soup and buttermilk cornbread for lunch. I've been hungry for that soup for a week, and just wouldn't make it because of the carbs. But I've been good all week, so I went for it. Gosh, it tasted so good.

Just about ready to upload my new non-fiction book..STEERING FROM THE BACKSEAT. I'm so excited. Waiting on the final cover for the print version and then I'm doing them all at once. Print, then digital. I'll definitely post when they show up on Amazon.

I miss Leslie Wainger. She was my editor at Harlequin/Mira for 24 years. I won't wish her back, because that would be selfish. She certainly earned her retirement, and I can only imagine how happy she is now. She always worked at the zoo near where she lived when she was working, and loved it so much. I know she retired near another zoo, so she's doing what gives her joy. But I miss her. Working with someone else isn't always easy. I've had my other editor now for 3 years and never met her. Have no feeling of rapport. It's just do the job, miscommunications, she doesn't know me. She has no basis of how to trust my work. It's like dating.... More stumbles than the heart will allow.

But that's life. Stuff happens. Things change. It is what it is.

The time between birth and death is an unknown.

Don't waste it with regrets.

Follow your heart.

Follow your instincts.

They'll keep you on your path.

❧

Each day brings new opportunity.

Look for it.

Take a different road to work.

It matters that you see something new each day.

Look into the eyes of the person with whom you are talking.

Really see them.

Hear them.

There is no such thing as a Road to Nowhere.

All roads lead somewhere.

All roads have a destination.

You chose the road and the destination by the choices you make.

When children speak, listen.

Their truth is uncolored by deception and lies.

Teach them early that you value their existence.

Show them how to be, by being the example.

Being rude is not a goal in life.

Don't take pride in what amounts to a character flaw.

Just because you are able to talk louder and longer, doesn't mean you deserve to be heard.

The analogy of a person who sees money in the gutter, but refuses to pick it up because of the dirt, is in equal proportion to a person in dire need of rescue from the gutter, but is deemed unworthy.

And yet the same person who walked past the money and the man, will buy and eat food that grew in dirt.

What the money, and the homeless, and the food had in common was simply help getting clean.

❧

In all ways...be kind.

Forgive.

Let go.

Grudges put weight on your heart that no amount of dieting will remove.

Hate toward others only poisons YOU.

Lying turns to guilt, which eats away at your peace of mind.

Apologize.

Accept apologies.

Make amends.

Settle grievances.

Don't teach your children to perpetuate meanness.

When you shame yourself, you are also shaming everyone who bears your name.

You shout, "It's my life. I can do what I want."

And the answer is..."Yes, yes, you CAN do that.

But before you act, ask yourself, 'Is there another way you can think of, to follow your heart without causing all of this damage among those you love?"

Just because you can, doesn't always mean you should.

Stay strong in your faith.

Stand in the light of right.

Don't be afraid to be different.

You don't have to go down with the sinking ship,

If you're already wearing a life jacket.

Use the brains you came with and do the right thing.

❧

Kids having fits in public, and then the parent giving in and giving them what they want to quiet them down, is probably the biggest shift in parenting from when I was a kid, and when i was raising my own.

As my Daddy used to say, "You stop that shit before it starts."

In other words, the first time it happens, should also be the last.

I remember the first time my little red-head, Kathy, had herself a fit. She was about four. We'd been visiting friends, and one of their children had decided to pitch a fit, and threw herself into the floor and started to cry, and then would hold her breath. I guess she'd done that once until she passed out. It had frightened the parents, and so they were prone to giving in so she wouldn't do that again. Yes, she got what she'd wanted, but they were trying to cope with a very scary scenario to them, but to my little squirt, she saw a possible, positive outcome in the fit, and the very next day, she pulled that stunt with me.

We were in the kitchen. It was nearing dinner time (noon) and I was cooking as fast as I could, knowing a hungry husband was going to show up at any moment demanding food, because he was in a hurry to get back to the field. My squirt wanted a cookie. I told her it was almost dinner time and just wait, and...nope... she wasn't having that. But instead of throwing herself forward into the floor, she carefully sat down, then stretched out on her back (I didn't raise no dummy) then proceeded to start flopping her hands and kicking and screaming and bawling. She couldn't work up the tears, but she was making a lot of noise.

I just keep working. She stopped. I turned around and looked at her. She started it up again. I ignored her. She stopped again. I turned around, carefully stepped over her to get a platter out of the other cabinet, and then said..."be careful down there, honey. Mama doesn't want to step on those little fingers," and then stepped back over her. She laid there a minute. I could feel those little eyes boring into my back, and then she jumped up, and wandered off into her room to play. She had many fits growing up, but never in public, and she darn sure didn't get a treat afterward.

Everyone comes with a different personality.

But we all have the same social moirés by which we live.

And now, when I see some kid having a big-ass fit in public, and I've seen some doozies...

I don't think that's a rotten kid.

I look at the parents, instead.

They're the ones who, 'let that shit happen."

❦

They were Vegan meatballs. Vegan.

Non-GMO...Organic...blah, blah, blah.

I can't have meat. So I gave them a try.

They were okay. I ate two little ones with some spaghetti and a little sauce. Two hours later I can't stand up on my left foot for the pain...as if I'd eaten real meatballs. wtf?

I go look at the packaging. A whole butt-load of stuff, and 14 grams of pea protein.

Evidently, I can no longer do fake meat, either.

No meat.

Next to no carbs.

No processed sugars.

I need a do-over on metabolism, and a filter put on my genetics.

You go along, minding your own business, until one day your body goes..

"Oh hell no! You can't have that anymore!"

And then puts you through seven levels of misery to prove it.

So I Googled the meds available for Gout. I Googled the meds available for RA. And then I read the warnings and side-effects on all of them, and said,

"Oh hell no. I'm not having that either."

I had about 70 years of eating what I wanted without being allergic to anything.

Now I'm afraid to hiccup, for what might come loose.

I think it's Life's way of proving that we never really were in charge.

That it is just lying in wait for the opportune time to tie one last knot in our tails.

❧

When I was a very little girl, I used to wish I was small enough to live under a toadstool. I would lay on my belly in the grass and get as close to one as I could, then rest my chin on my hands and envision me...there...

I saw the possibilities...I believed it could happen if I wished it hard enough. Tiny chair, tiny bed. Tiny shelf with a bowl of tiny berries. Little Spider was a friend, and she wove me a web that was so fine, that the spaces between her stitches disappeared, and she gave it to me for a rug for my floor. At night I would get my blanket from the tiny thimble where I stored it, then unroll it and climb into bed.

I could see stars out the window..Oh...didn't I tell you there were walls? I meant to, because they were there. Anyway...I couldn't go to sleep until I saw the shooting star. I saw it every night, and once I did, it was safe to go to sleep, because I believed that the rider on that star was coming to take me home.

I look back on that now and see two things.

One: I hadn't been here long enough to forget where I'd come from.

Two: Being tiny meant being invisible, which meant I was hidden from the turmoil in our home.

Such innocence, and already wrapped up in ways to sail through this muggle life without going under.

I don't see me beneath toadstools anymore.

My spirit stands tall on the path I now walk.

But I still look to the stars...every night...

Waiting for the rider on that star.

❧

I've been busy today.

Yard guy mowed.

It's trash day.

Errands to run, then almost an hour long, work-related conference call, then a quick trip down Highway 9, and now I'm home.

It is hot.

Clouds above are so big, like the kind that build into thunderstorms, but none are predicted.

I'm sailing right along on my WIP and ready to sit down with my feet and get back to work on it.

I am staying in a place of positive thinking, because it matters more that I do that. It keeps me on a peaceful path, and it keeps the energy of much needed light ablaze.

What is made with love, and gifted with a generous heart, is more valuable than what money can buy.

Lust isn't love.

Loneliness can't be cured with love.

You must first love yourself.

You must value yourself.

Just because you want to be in love,

Does not guarantee success.

What is said between you in the beginning means nothing.

Most often, what is said is what they think you want to hear.

That's how they hook you.

Questions you should be asking yourself.

What is his past about? Not what he's told you, but what you know for sure.

Where does he work? If the answer is nowhere, he's looking for a woman to take care of him.

Never bring what amounts to a stranger into your home if there are children with you.

It's one thing to take a chance on your own well-being, but you don't have the right to put the children in harm's way.

Don't be desperate.

Be smart.

You might be wondering where this all came from, so I'll share.

A story on the news...

It was from a past crime, but the man...the killer...was just now being sentenced.

Woman and family dead...because she let the devil she didn't know in the door.

&

Tomorrow is Kathy's birthday.

She requested Enchilada Casserole and a big tossed salad. Dessert request was even easier. A slice of carrot cake from La Baguette...A slice of Cheesecake for Ash, and whatever I want. LOLOLOL

So this morning...you know what I was doing...Yep. One quick trip to La Baguette, another trip to Homeland to get the stuff, and I'm home.

Got a phone call late last night from my Little Mama's care center. She fell again. They called her Hospice care to come check her. Bump on the back of her head. Tiny little cut they patched up. They gave her a glass of milk, and put her to bed. They said she was asleep within seconds.

I have nothing to say that hasn't been said before, except I didn't sleep much last night. And so it is.

There will be a time in life that you will remember forever.

A time that might come only once.

When you realize that, in that moment, everything you are is in alignment with the Universe.

When you are so aware of life in all its forms, that you can hear the tiny sounds, the sounds that are always beneath the noise.

When you feel your heart beating in rhythm to the vibration of the earth on which you stand.

When you know that, if you shut your eyes and inhaled, you could fly.

That's your soul...showing itself in that brief, flash of cognizance, letting you know that you are more than you understand, that you have strength you've never used, and knowledge gained down through the ages.

It is the shooting star in your life...that moment of understanding...and then it's gone.

You may never remember it...or understand the importance of what you just experienced.

But I am telling you now...no matter what heartaches or trouble you are experiencing, you are a being of light and love.

꙳

Last night I dreamed in color.

I don't always notice it in dreams, but I did last night.

I was in a place that I'd never been before--a big white, two story house, with a glassed-in sun porch, set in a wide rural panorama of beauty.

The view from either floor, and from any window, was either rolling farmland, or homes similar to mine, visible in the distances.

I was working at the sink when I glanced up and saw a man, either husband or hired hand, working on a piece of machinery that had broken down at the edge of the field just beyond the white fences (the kind that are made of PVC material, in the back yard. It was a hot, windless day...like the ones that wring the moisture straight out of your body, leaving you weak and shaking.

As I watched, something the man was doing sparked a fire. The first little licks of flame showed up beneath the machinery, and he was trying to stomp it out when it caught in the dry grass around him.

Then a tiny whirlwind, no more than ten or twelve feet high, sprang up out of nowhere, picked up the flames, and carried them across my fence, and into the yard.

I was screaming and running for the phone, but it had no dial tone. I ran to look for my cell phone, but it had no power, either. I ran back into the kitchen, saw the fence melting in the fire, and the man beyond, afire on the ground...and the swiftly burning flames were at the porch.

I ran out of the house as fast as I could, and didn't look back until I was standing on a hill some distance away.

As I turned, looking through the windows on the sun porch, I could see flames eating away at the interior of my house, like termites taking down wood.

I was crying.

The whole valley was now ablaze...the houses I could see in the distance were on fire, the dry pasture lands were burning.

It was as if someone had taken a blowtorch to the world, and it was burning down before my eyes.

I looked behind me and saw I was encircled in flames, and in that instant, all fear disappeared. I was suddenly calm, accepting of my fate.

Just as the flames were licking at my feet, the alarm went off.

Saved by the bell.

I was still in a state of acceptance when I got out of bed. I think it was a message to me, that no matter what I had imagined was going to happen to me...it did not...because I didn't resist.

Sometimes when we are going through hard times and troubled times, our fear of what might...is far worse than what is...and the more we feed fear, the stronger it becomes.

Trust the process of life, knowing this, too, shall pass.

§

The hill was steep.

The ruts were deep.

The earth was dark red clay.

The rain that came the night before had turned it into a snotty slide going down, and an impossibility going up.

Not even the tires on Daddy pickup--the ones he called ground grips--were making any headway. He'd get about halfway up that hill, gunning the engine like he was about to take off from the flight deck of a Navy aircraft carrier.

And every time, the back end of that pickup would first slide sideways, then the whole truck followed, sliding sideways right back down the hill, with Daddy cussing a blue streak all the way down.

And how, you might ask, do I know this?

Because I, at the age of eleven, was riding in the seat beside him.

The top of that hill was only a few yards from the gate that led straight to Grand and Grampy's outbuildings...and the barn where Daddy needed to unload the sacks of calf feed that were in the truck bed.

Frankly, I was getting weary of the death slide, because I thought every time we started to slide, the next step would be when we began to roll.

I wanted out.

"What are we gonna do, Daddy?"

"Hell if I know, sweetie," he said.

And then we both heard Grampy starting up his Poppin' Johnny, that's what they called old-time John Deere tractors.

Daddy pulled his handkerchief from his pocket and wiped the sweat off his face.

"Sounds like Grampy might be coming to our rescue," he said.

We both looked up that steep hill just as Grampy and his tractor came into view.

"Hallelujah," Daddy muttered, as we watched that old tractor come right down that hill as if it was hard-packed earth, and pass us as he went farther down to turn around. A couple of minutes later, Grampy came rolling right past us again, then stopped.

He was grinning when he got out of the tractor, and Daddy could laugh now at our predicament, too. I watched from inside the pickup, as they hooked a log chain beneath the front bumper.

Grampy got back in the tractor. Daddy got back in with me.

And the ride up began...this time with success.

The wheels on Grampy's tractor were the kind that looked like giant cogs, before rubber tires. Those big iron wheels rolled right on up that hill, those big cogs digging right down in that wet, red earth and pulling us up, as easy as flying a kite.

By the time we got up the hill and towed into the barn lot, Daddy's pickup was covered in clumps of red clay, from those cogs had dug up and thrown back on us.

"I'm going to the house," I said, and cleared out of the pickup, knowing Grand would have something cold for me to drink, and most likely a cookie.

Once the truck was unloaded, they hosed the mud off at the calf lot. When Daddy was ready to go, he drove up to the house and honked. I came out running, carrying two cookies wrapped in waxed paper for him.

Daddy grinned when he saw them, and ate the first one in two bites, then looked at me and winked.

"Mmm, it was worth getting stuck to eat some of Grand's cookies, right honey?"

I hesitated. "Almost," I said.

He started laughing, and then ate the last cookie as we headed home.

By the time we pulled into the yard at our house, he was whistling Yankee Doodle.

Daddy was quick to anger.

Food calmed the savage beast in him.

But I think whistling soothed his soul.

He's been gone from this earth for a long, long time, but while he was here, he was larger than life.

And when I was little, I saw the world from Daddy's shoulders.

It looked vast to me then.

I think of where he is now and can only imagine what a view it must be,

Living among the stars.

§

People are always going to see an event from their own perspective.

Being horrified at their reaction is pointless.

They likely think the same about you.

Be you and move along.

We have been at war on this planet for thousands of years. THOU-SANDS of years...And yes, battles have been won, but not the wars. Wars are never resolved. They are always on a back burner, with the losers simmering, and the winners gloating in a false bubble of security. Nothing was resolved. Understanding never happened. It was simply a case of being conquered...or conquering. Despite the outer reasons for battle...it's always about power. Somebody has what someone else wants.

That is a pathetic example of humanity.

We all come from the same source...we are bits of light from the great I AM. The way we look here, is how we chose to look. The ethnicity we chose to live out in this life, was for a purpose. There is always a reason behind the obvious, and yet we...these perfect parts of

God...still manage to disgrace ourselves, lifetime after lifetime, in constant battle.

Some of our favorite pastimes involve men fighting with each other for sport. Blood spurts from a cut eye. Someone is knocked unconscious, or someone is so battered and broken they are carried off the field of play, and we watch the violence and carnage, like Romans in an amphitheater, waiting for the lions to devour the losers.

If we don't have a world war to fight, we'll just fight about religion, or with our neighbors. We lie, we cheat, we steal, we fight.

We are selfish. We belittle. We humiliate. We embarrass. We have lost every holy aspect of the soul within us, in an effort to be better than. To be the best one.

We don't have sports for the joy of it.

We have winners and losers.

Don't you see how divisive this is?

Do you understand the pervasive undertone of "I am better than you"?

Does it ever...EVER...occur to you to just stop it?

Do you always have to be right?

Being born is a gift. It does not mean a fight for the right to exist

&.

The amount of baking I do is in direct response to my need to fix the world.

So since I can only work on me, I baked.

I got the recipe from FB. Dear lord, what a mistake.

I'm not a huge lover of cake, so I thought it would be safe. I could bake, give it away, and all would be well.

Except the name of the recipe was deceiving.

Apple Dapple cake.

Sounds innocent enough, right?

Jesus Take The Wheel.

It is, without doubt, the moistest, best, caramel tasting, apple and pecan filled cake I ever had in my life.

If I can find it again, I'll just share. Otherwise I'll have to post it myself because...well...you know how much I love you guys, and I could never be selfish enough not to share this one.

I have to get this out of my house as fast as I can. I ate one piece. Probably shot the hell out of my blood sugar test tomorrow morning. And I was doing so good.

Tomorrow I'm cutting it up, sending a bunch of it to Kathy, and the rest home with Crissy and Courtney when they stop by tomorrow.

None of this would be necessary if we could all just get along.

Stress bakers understand.

I got fat once because my marriage was miserable.

I'm not doing that again, no matter how bad ya'll behave...got it?

I'm going to look for that recipe...taking a picture of my cake, minus the piece I ate, to go with it, and putting it on a separate post.

Knock yourself out.

APPLE DAPPLE CAKE

3 cups all purpose flour
  1 teaspoon salt
  1 teaspoon baking soda
  1 cup chopped pecans
  1 cup vegetable oil
  2 cups of sugar
  3 eggs
  2 teaspoons of vanilla
  3 cups of raw apples, peeled and chopped fine

SAUCE:
  1 cup packed brown sugar
  1/4 cup milk
  3/4 cup butter or margarine

For cake: Mix oil, sugar, eggs, and vanilla. Sift together, flour, salt, and soda. Add dry ingredients to wet ingredients and mix well. Fold in pecans and apples. Bake in tube or Bundt pan at 350 degrees for 1 hour.

For Sauce: mix and cook ingredients until it comes to a boil, then cook ingredients 3 minutes at a gentle boil, stirring constantly. Pour over hot cake while cake is still in pan. Let cake cool completely before removing.

It was hard to get out of the Bundt pan, even though I prepared it well. Next time I'll use a tube pan. FYI

❧

Appearance.
    Not how you're dressed.
    Not the skillfully applied makeup.
    Not the house you live in.
    Not the car you drive.

Reality.
    How you behave toward others.
    Genuine empathy.
    A loving heart.
    Goes with the flow in a change of plans.

Warning signals.
    Road rage.
    Lies.
    Repeatedly expecting you to sacrifice.
    Selfishness.
    Job hopper.
    No job at all.

Deceptive.
    Eyes reveal the depth of a smile.
    A hand out, means less than a hand up.

Promises that never materialize.

Too many secrets.

Acceptance.

This is your right.

You accept into your circle of friends and acquaintances...only the people with whom you feel safe.

It is not your job to rehabilitate everyone you meet.

Our world is changing drastically by the day.

We're long past the time of giving someone the benefit of the doubt.

The in-between world and the people in it no longer exist.

You are either standing in the light.

Or you're with the others.

Pick a side and hang on.

The ride is going to get rougher.

❧

Did you ever see a magnificent tree in all its glory, and want to climb it...to be beneath the majesty of ancient limbs and verdant leaves, so thick you couldn't see up through them to the sky?

Believing that if you got to the top, you would know the secrets to life?

Have you ever climbed up a tree without thought of how high you would go, and then got about halfway up and became scared?

If you kept climbing, it would be higher than you'd ever gone.

You hesitated, and looked up. Then you turned your head and looked down. You didn't know what was up there, but you knew what was below.

This is called a crossroad. You have many of them in life.

You are diddling through days without thought of what you did with them, in a rut, but too careful to step out.

Then an opportunity comes to you, and at first you are ecstatic. But the closer you get to change, the more afraid you become.

It's that old saying of... 'better the devil you know, than the one you don't'.

So you changed your mind and went back.

You were halfway up that tree and climbed down.

And missed the gift the Universe offered, then lived the rest of your life with regret...wondering what might have happened if you had stepped out...if you'd climbed higher.

The Universe only asks one thing of us...to believe, and live within that belief of faith.

It's called The Leap.

You've all heard the phrase, leap of faith.

So, we are being asked daily now, to trust in the Light...trust in the Good. To not engage in what only amounts to verbal warfare, which solves NOTHING.

You don't have to believe me.

But you do need to believe in yourself.

The next time you come to a crossroad...take it.

༺

I had a day dream coming home from church this morning. That's what I call the little 'visions' that pop into my head. They're part of the messages I get that I'm supposed to share, and for whatever reason, today there is someone who needs to see and understand life from this perspective. And...if you don't believe, then move along. I am only a messenger.

So...for whomever needs to read this to better process the passing of a loved one.

This is the vision, from me, and Spirit to you.

Many bright, glittering lights of the Great I Am, which we call souls, were in a gathering place, readying for a return to Earth for a new life.

One is asking another--"what will your purpose be this time around?" The other responds--"Ultimately, I will be homeless. It is part of a life lesson for me, because I got lost in the accumulation of property and power in my last life and became selfish. So I will live life from the other perspective this time, to gain knowledge and to heal the harm I did before. What is yours?"

"Oh, my trip will be very short. I won't be human long. I will be helping a member of my soul family, who desires more empathy, compassion, and understanding, so I will incarnate as one of their family, and die young. I'll be home soon."

Another soul listening, added yet another purpose. "I will live a life of poverty in this life, because in my last lifetime, I lost my way, and stole money from good people, and did not attend to the purpose for which I'd come."

And yet another soul chimed in. "I will be female in this lifetime. I have lived many lives as male, and always betrayed the women I loved. My purpose this time will be a woman who is betrayed. In this way, I will understand the depth of damage I have caused in past lives.

And so it went. As quickly as they each transitioned to their birth, other souls came forward, each with their own lessons to learn and purposes to fulfill, each choosing the life in which to learn it...and accepting that, no matter how hard it is for others they leave behind, when they have finished their soul contract, they will be welcomed home with great joy, back into the soul families from which they came.

At this point, the vision ended.

I know it is very difficult to come from the viewpoint of a human, to grasp this...that there are real reasons as to why we are born a certain way, and why we die.

I have grieved as you have, without understanding. I have been angry, and lost faith. We all come from different religions or no religions at all, and we believe what we've been taught, unless it felt foreign to us from the start and we already knew to seek broader meanings.

But then these truths have been shown to me, and as I've lived with this knowledge, it has truly made losing loved ones easier to bear. Yes, I still grieve, but I also realize they rejoice, as they go home. I always picture it as a homecoming, and imagine the joy and welcome they receive.

Spirit needs you to know these truths.

No one's death is an accident.

No disease is because of something you did, or is, in any way, a punishment.

Nobody dies too young.

Nobody is lucky they're living to old age.

When their soul contract is up--when they've come to do what they intended, even if they did it wrong--they will transition back to spirit.

They're not being cheated out of life.

They GET to go home.

Yes, they know that the people who love them will grieve, but you have to remember, sometimes their passing is FOR other people's life lessons--the ones they cannot learn until they suffer the losses.

The disasters we face, the terror, the illness, the loneliness, the betrayals....OR the perfect lives some live, while others have no homes at all....are all part of the plan.

The lesson isn't always how you survive...but that you DID survive...and that you learned.

Life is life, until it's over.

We're only here for a little while.

⁊❧

I learned a long time ago that life wasn't like my Grand's kitchen. That life wouldn't hand me every answer for the bleeding cut on my knee, the hunger for a cookie, the soft breasts to lay my head on when I cried, the arms that held me through the storm.

The love within that kitchen that was emanating from her, was palpable. I could feel better, just by being there.

As I grew older, it became obvious that the blood will stop flowing on a scratch, that the hunger in my belly would be assuaged by something other than what I wanted, that I often cried alone, and weathered storms by facing them head on, daring life to stop me.

I knew my persona did not reflect the warrior within.

I was the shy one. The quiet one. The one who turned the other cheek. Until I didn't.

The day came when it became evident there was something I needed to survive, that no one could provide for me.

I had to do it for myself.

It's hard to change. You have to stop worrying about what family thinks. What your friends think. What the people at church thought. What the neighbors thought.

They hadn't walked on your path.

They had no idea of your life experiences, and their soul was not like your soul.

My soul sister was smothered in what I'd let happen to her.

She was shouting into my subconscious... "You have forgotten why you came. You are drowning yourself in despair. You have denied yourself joy in the name of duty. You are letting other people run your life, just because it's easier.

YOU DIDN'T COME HERE FOR EASY.

YOU CAME HERE TO WORK.

And that, in a nutshell, is how we let being human detract us from what we came here to do.

This is not how I imagined my life. It is certainly not how I expected to grow old.

But once you remember you are more than what's now...that you've been here and gone, through so many human experiences...and you realize the waste you have left in your wake...it makes doing it right this time, even more important.

You can talk all day about why you can't.

And I can counter ever reason for why you can.

Saying you have responsibilities to others first, is the easy way to stay at the same tasks.

You don't have to leave where you are to change.

You don't even have to go down the block to find something new.

Life presents opportunities on a daily basis.

The thing is...YOU have to be looking to see them.

Complacent is not the starter button you need to be pushing when you're looking for a new way of being in the world.

Change means growth.

And the only thing holding you back, is you.

৵

Rules on the Courtesy of Borrowing:

When I was a kid and living in the country in Oklahoma, there was a routine to asking a neighbor to borrow something.

It could be asking to borrow the services of a herd bull for your cows, or a piece of equipment, or their fishing boat...whatever.

So, when you did this, you loaded up the wife and kids and drove to the neighbor's house.

Everyone gets out of the pickup. The women go into the house, the kids go off to play, and the men stay outside, take a position around the bed of the pickup, facing the interior and each other, and talk. That way, they can spit all they want (men don't swallow their spit, but I don't know why) and talk about what's new in town, how their crops are growing, remarking upon the very pregnant hound underneath the shade tree, and telling the owner when she whelps, that you'd like one of the males because your hunting dog won't hunt with you anymore due to the buckshot you accidentally put in his butt.

The wife comes out on the porch, shades her eyes as she looks toward the truck, and calls out..."I need to be gettin' back. I got tomatoes to can."

He waves to acknowledge he heard her, and they talk for thirty more minutes.

One of the kids suddenly shrieks out in pain. It's one of yours, thank God, which means your kid didn't hurt the neighbor's kid, and your wife comes out again, this time with her hands on her hips, and just stares her husband down. He waves again to indicate he gets it, and then the two men talk for twenty more minutes.

The wife comes out with her kids and gets in the truck without talking.

The men look at each other and laugh. Then the men shake

hands...they say it's been good talking to you... and as the farmer is getting in the truck to go home, he stops with one foot on the running board, and says... "Hey, if you ain't using your hay rake tomorrow, can I borrow it for the day?"

The neighbor nods. "Sure thing. It's out behind the barn, if I'm not here."

And then you drive away.

કે

I had lunch with Scout today. He called to invite me last night. It was a thing to look forward to, today.

As we were eating, I said, "I can't believe you're going to be a Junior when school starts."

He said, "I can't believe school is starting again."

I laughed and told him it's way easier to go to school than it is to get up and go to work every day. At school, you get to pick who you do and don't want to hang out with. At work, you will have to work with people you don't like, and do it without complaining.

"I guess," he said.

LOL

It's all about the perception.

Anyway...I'm home.

My bra is off.

My shoes are off.

TMI?

Sorry. Not sorry. :-)

I just finished off a glass of ice tea.

And I want a nap.

Instead, I'm going to work, because...as I just told Scout, adults go to work, even if they'd rather take a nap.

I woke up with the words..."People get ready...there's a train a' comin'...going through my mind, and I am humming the melody without conscious thought.

When that is the first thing out of my mouth when I open my eyes,

I know it is something I was told on my spirit walk last night... and it's something I am to remember.

So, I'm ready...I'm always ready for change.

If there's something coming that takes me forward in life, "I'll just get on board."

Whatever it may be, I'm in it, on it, with it, doing it, and not afraid to be there.

☙

Have patience.

But I don't. Not much.

Why do you continue to doubt us?

I am afraid.

Do you understand faith?

Yes. You believe without the need of physical proof.

Do you have faith?

Yes.

In us?

I sigh. Yes. Always.

Then don't be afraid. You are never alone.

I know. I feel your presence.

Then feel also, our love for you.

Yes. I am sorry for the doubt.

Sorry is not necessary. Faith is.

Being human is so hard.

Of course it is, warrior. It is why you were chosen. You know what you need.

Yes. I have faith. I need Patience.

And so it is.

For all of you today:

Stand in the light and don't look back

☙

Kathy and Ash just brought me a mess of purple hull peas and some little cucumbers from Farmer's Market. She knows I like the little ones to slice and eat. I'll have purple fingers for the day, but it'll be worth it. They are my favorite kind of field pea.

Knowing that you are thought of, and that your feelings are considered, is a blessing.

I've been eating some watermelon almost every day. It tastes pretty good right now...but I don't buy a whole one. I always wind up throwing part of it away because I can't eat it all before it turns yucky. And buying a piece of one already cut open is also a pretty good way for me to get a good one. I haven't gotten a dud yet.

It was supposed to rain last night. And the wind was going to blow so hard. yada yada yada... So I took my bird feeder off the perch and just set it up under the patio last night so the bird seed wouldn't be ruined. Only it didn't rain. It didn't even fart up a good breeze. And I overslept. And the birds found the feeder anyway because....birds...and so I walk outside this morning to hang it back on the hook and laughed out loud.

Do birds have toga parties?

Do you think there are orgies in the bird world?

From the amount of poop and bird seed scattered all over the place, it sure looked like it.

First thing I did this morning...hosed off the back patio.

The feeder is on the hook and my patio is no longer the scene of a crime.

I know nothing officer. I slept through the whole thing.

SOMETHING TO THINK ABOUT:

We throw away food and let others go hungry. We discard the elderly. We leave the indigent on the streets. We funnel children into social services and then forget they're there.

We let people tell us what to do, where to go, how to behave, what to eat, what not to eat, what we should wear. They tell us we're too young, but will send us to war.. They tell us we're too old to work and retire us...then complain because of the help we need afterward. We aren't a consideration, until we have something they want.

We are rats in the maze, running toward the cheese, or starting a fight, every time we are triggered. We've been conditioned and we react accordingly.

Who, you might ask, are, They? Who do you mean when you say, We? When I say You, are you talking to me?

YES. I'm talking to you, me, we, they.

This is the year 2018. And this is our nation as we know it today.

And THIS is not okay.

ॐ

A child who stands back may not be shy, but cautious.

They are the watchers, judging situations and the people in them, before they make a decision as to whether they might be a part of their tribe.

Don't push them forward, assuming you are doing them a favor by inserting them into a group.

Children have more discernment than their parents when it comes to people.

If your child repeatedly shies away from someone, heed that sign. They can spot a fake within moments of meeting them.

Children see past smiles. They hear false laughter. They sense the deception, without knowing the word for it.

Pay attention.

They are the weather vanes, the security alarms, the guardians that you don't even know you need.

ॐ

Having lunch with Scout today before he heads north to his grandpa's house to stay the week. He's hardly been here this summer. I know his Mama has sure missed him, but now it's past time that they'll be doing anything together except going back to school.

Kathy has already started working in her classroom even though school won't start for a few weeks. Such is the life of a teacher. I bought lunch for myself after church yesterday, and while I was waiting to pick it up, she called, asked what I was doing, and I wound up eating my lunch at the house with her, rather than taking it home by myself. She was already laminating things for school. The best part, she's so excited to go back to class. After so many years of teaching pre-K and Kindergarten, she is teaching second grade and loves it.

Work isn't work when you look forward to each day.

That's how I feel about writing.

§

Last night was such a blessing for us. We had an all-out thunderstorm, but without the damaging wind and hail that was present in other parts of the state. I don't know how much rain, but it was a good toad-soaker, as my Grampy used to say.

Adjusting:

It's what we do when things don't always fit what we expected.

Taking things and people for granted:

You never know you're doing it, until the opportunity, or the people, have passed away.

Saying what you think without consideration for others:

My first thought is always, WHY?

Being inappropriate:

Juvenile behavior.

Being a bully:

Only cowards do it.

If the Universe gives back to you,

That which you say...

Then cursing someone else,

Means you have first damned yourself in the name of God,

Or asked to be defiled, in the name of your mother.

What you say,

Is what you get.

§

I woke up with this, to be shared with you.

A heart can break, when breath has ceased.

But it doesn't change all the love in me.

I can grieve, I can weep, as I stand at your grave

But it doesn't change all the love you gave.

This is as honest a statement that can be made about life, love, loss, and living again.

And we do live again in a whole new way.

It's how life works. It's what we're supposed to do.

We love many times in life. Some last. Some don't.

But the loss is always painful at some level.

What we miss...what is often misunderstood, is that love is not just the emotion between two people...or within a family.

Love is what grows our light, grows our capacity to empathize, grows the humanity in all of us.

Treasure the gift while it is in your life, and release the passing with gratitude, knowing that, for a certain space and time, everything that mattered was given to you.

Love once given, is forever yours.

Even if you reject it later. Even if it is taken away without your consent.

It is forever a part of who you were then, and goes with you into who you are now.

Don't cry for what's gone.

Take strength from what is.

Love made you weep,

But it's still yours to keep.

჻

First day of August. School begins soon. I swear every kid in town was in my dentist's office getting teeth cleaned.

Comments from up and down the halls were hysterical.

One little girl kept saying...He's gonna fall outa dat chair.

Another one was disapproving of the process.

Mothers comments were hysterical, too.

I heard a piece of one conversation from my dental chair..."Yes, I'm here with all four kids.." then her voice trailed off. She might have been on the verge of tears. LOL

The waiting room was busy, too, kids were everywhere.

Good for business, but I'll bet those dental techs go home freakin' exhausted, and parents will be eating mac and cheese and beans for a month to pay for it all.

My dental hygienist was so nice. She was super careful about not hurting me because I told her I was a big baby...even covered me up with a blanket because I was cold, and yet I sat in my chair and kept forgetting to breathe.

They always do a pre-check for swollen lymph glands, etc...and, as she was feeling along my jaw and down the side of my neck, she kept commenting about how firm it was. I said, "That's awesome. I didn't know there was anything firm left on my body."

Made her laugh.

I even had my choice of flavors of the fluoride they put on my teeth at the end. It was Mint, Caramel, or Birthday Cake, or something to that effect. I shuddered, and chose Mint. Can't imagine having a caramel or cake flavored coating on my teeth for two hours. Not unless I was eating the real thing. LOL

I didn't get a sticker for being good, but I did get a to-go bag. Even dentists have to-go bags. New toothbrush..toothpaste...dental floss, etc.

One cleaning over. Mint flavor on my teeth, and a to-go bag. All for the low, retail price of $238.00.

Oh... and a repeat performance just for me.

I have to go back at the end of the month to get a filling repaired.

When I lived on the farm, we could always just sell a calf to pay for this stuff.

Now I'm without livestock of any kind.

Anybody want to buy some books?

HOT JULY SUMMER

I could have just called this July, and everyone in the state of Oklahoma would already know that meant hot. We're enjoying (I say that with just the tiniest bit of sarcasm) triple digit heat. Ugh, and thank God for whoever invented air conditioning, because it was non-existent when I was a kid. I remember the first water-cooler my family bought. We thought it was a miracle, but it did get a little crowded standing right in front of it where the air was the coolest.

Bedtime during those years meant plenty of hot sleepless nights. We used to pray for a breeze, or an unexpected thunderstorm, just to cool things off. My sister and I would lie motionless on our backs, our arms out-flung, hoping to catch even the tiniest wisp of stirring air. When our parents finally bought an old circulating fan, we took turns lying on the side of the bed closest to it, and we made a rule that no one slept on their side, because that would block the air. It was either on your tummy or on your back.

When the days got hot, it meant playing in the shade instead of out in the yard. We still played, regardless of weather. Where does that wonderful abandon go as we get older? Do we trade creature comforts for joy? I hope not. I still remember what it feels like to run barefoot through hot sand, and the utter bliss of flying down the hillside toward the creek, knowing what that cool water was going to feel like on my hot bare feet.

Life was so simple then. The sun came up. We did our chores and played. The sun went down. We did our chores and went to bed. The orchestrated 'play dates' parents make for their children now often leave me speechless. Play should not be on a schedule for anyone under the age of ten. It should be an inalienable right, and batteries are not included.

But those days are nothing but fond memories. All I would wish back from those times are my father and my sister. They've been gone for far too many years. Still, sometimes when the air is so hot that it burns the inside of my nose just to take a breath, I can almost hear my sister laughing as she would beat me to the creek; watching the water splashing up on the back of her legs and the joy on her face as she turned around and yelled. "I won!"

Yes, she beat me at just about everything. I imagine her now--never still--never quiet—and that clear, perfect laugh, ringing out all over heaven.

§⋙

I spent a good portion of yesterday evening in my back yard, raking pine needles up into piles. That thunderstorm we had last week blew the whole yard full of them, and today was my yard guy's day to mow. I told him I managed to get them raked, but apologized because my foot and ankle were too sore to walk anymore, and he said he'd bag them up before he mowed..and he did.

I don't appreciate those fifty feet tall pine trees just across my fence. I said, fifty feet, but they could be taller. Anyway...they drop pine cones year round, and needles when there's a strong wind. Did I mention I dislike those trees?

I'm not a good judge of distance looking up, but I can mark off a quarter of a mile in my mind, and then do it, usually only a few yards off one way or another. "Country Girl skills." I've helped measure acres and acres of wheat or peanut land, walking it with a chain and stakes. Now, they have a better process.

But, I can't hang a picture straight to save my soul, I can't write straight across an unlined sheet of paper. All my writing goes uphill. I just made Pioneer Woman Lemon Rosemary scones, and no two are alike in size. LOL

I made them for Scout. He's been at his grandpa's all week and coming home tonight. He called me last night, and after I said Hello, I asked him what he was doing. He said he was watching the Pioneer Woman make those Lemon Rosemary Scones again. I laughed and told him that's what I was watching, too. Then I asked...is this call a request for me to make those again? He said, yes. I told him I'd have them waiting for him when he got home tonight. He said, in a happy tone of voice, Yay. Thank you."

I just took them out of the oven. As soon as they're completely cool, I'll glaze them. I'll face all the dirty dishes and pans later.

§.

Kathy invited me to lunch today. We went to La Madeline's in NorthPark, which is the new shopping area on the north side of town. We had the best time and the food was amazing. Our last hoorah of summer. School begins here soon.

Today was a day for getting things done, and tonight I'll write another chapter before I go to bed, because that has to be done, too.

Life is not about just living/existing.

Being human is about facing challenges every day.

Some are difficult. Some make us stop and think.

And some are all about repairing the errors of our way.

It's hard to watch people you love making horrible choices, that in the end, you know good and well, will destroy them.

However...remember why we're here.

To learn. To grow.

Accepting a truth that some souls actually come here TO FAIL, seems ridiculous, but it's all about growing empathy and love.

So when you see a friend, or a family member, doing things you know are going to kill them, or at the least, send them to jail...if they're grown, unless they want to change, no amount of fighting, praying, hard love choices you make on their behalf, is going to change the ultimate outcome.

What you have to remember is...it's their path, not yours.

Bankrupting you...letting the stress and fear ruin your health, because you're worrying about someone else's life, is counterproductive.

Unless of course you'd rather go down with them, screaming and crying that you were right all along.

§♠

Open your heart.

Be ready to receive.

Blessings come daily. Some are small, and we often overlook them...thinking to ourselves..."oh, that's nice."

What you don't understand is...that nice thing was heaven-sent, and your gratitude, or lack thereof, was noted.

Why do we think that, only the noted gifts...the noteworthy events...the awards received...the money...the showy parts of our lives are the only things of note?

When you brag about your children in front of them, is it only when they've done something of note?

Have you ever praised a child for doing things without being told? For the kindness they show to others. For their moral support during hard times. For the blessings they are in your life, for no other reason than they exist?

Praising your children...or your mate...telling them how blessed you are that they are in your life, is what a layer of varnish is to wood. It seals in the beauty, and protects it from the weathering and troubles in life.

It can be the single reason that helps people you love stay on the right path.

When they know how cherished and appreciated they are by the people who love them, it's easier to say no, when the wrong people try to pull you onto their darker paths.

When I was a girl growing up, I was always in the kitchen with the women making the meal. Not because they needed a pair of extra hands, but because those women fed more than my hunger. They fed my soul.

"Sherry, would you wash this lettuce for me, honey? You always do such a good job of getting it clean."

"Sherry always sets such a pretty table... even when we're only laying out the everyday dishes."

"Sherry made that crust today, and it's just as good as mine."

"Oh, Sherry, thank you for doing those dishes. I don't know what's wrong with me, but I'm so tired today. I don't know what I would do without you."

Those simple praises and so many more, came from my Mother, my Grand, my Auntie, my Grandma Smith... from all the women in my life, who had a hand in making me who I am today.

And it wasn't just the praise that stuck with me. It was the trust and the love that came with it.

Be that person for the young ones in your lives.

Words matter, but it's the lack of them that changes who they were meant to be.

໒ຊ

I send the love in me to the need in you.

Let it lift your spirit and fill the void you are unable to fill for yourself.

Knowledge, intelligence, acuity, skill, aptitude, gifted: Words that describe people we look to when we are seeking answers, or needing help.

But there is no amount of knowledge that can replace the power of one single act of love.

The energy of the earth vibrates at 528 HZ, which is the same energy as Love.

Everything in the universe is energy in different frequencies.

Everything on earth holds its own vibration, from something as simple as a single blade of grass, to the greatest of all....the birth of a child.

Even if a child is born unwanted by humanity, it is a gift and a blessing from God, of God, given breath by God, and that is a love more powerful than anything created by man.

You move through life seeking acceptance, seeking recognition, wanting more than you need, wasting energy on gathering awards of your accomplishments in an effort to grow more power, because there is an emptiness within you that is yet to be filled. You don't know what it is...you never gave it a name...you didn't realize it was something that money can't buy, but it was love.

All you needed was love.

❧

Today: Hair appt.

Appt with Leslie.

Appt with Scout to take him clothes shopping for school. Writing...whenever the heck I can fit it in. LOLOL

Timing is everything, they say.

Timing is not always my friend.

I run on Me time.

It's the internal clock that I came with, and it is constantly being reprogrammed to accommodate my life, because that's more important to me, than perfection of every other thing.

I will always choose people first.

Clean houses come later.

Try one new thing today.

Lift one person up who is sad.

Step out of your rut at least once a day, even if it's nothing bigger than choosing a blueberry muffin instead of a banana muffin.

You think I'm making a joke?

Well, I'm not.

How will you grow if you don't allow yourself the freedom to be?

Step out of yourself.

Choose you.

❧

An apology is meant to be a sincere comment, made to someone else for what you've said or done, that hurt them.

Sometimes the hurt happens in total innocence.

Sometimes the hurt is premeditated and mean.

The thing is...regardless of how it happened, the injured party is still in physical or emotional pain.

The first thing to do, in order to repair what is done, is to apologize sincerely.

A snide twist to the words, I'm sorry, does not count.

That is just another dig into what's already been said.

But when the apology is truly remorseful, and given in sincerity, then that is truly all that can be done from your standpoint.

From that day on, your guilt in the hurtful words..or whatever was said or done...is no longer yours.

If people choose to hold onto anger and grudges, despite the other party wanting to make peace, then that is their right.

Your job then, is to step out of the choice they've made.

You are no longer part of the equation.

They have chosen to fight a lonely war.

Live like today is the best day of your life, even if it's not.

The simple act of giving joy, often brings it to you.

☙

When I was a little girl, people still visited. They didn't call. Nobody had phones. They just showed up, usually around noon, with the whole family, and no one got upset. No one freaked out.

My Grampy would look out and say..."Here come the Donathans, or the Davises are here, or that looks like Rippy's old truck.

And Grand would say, is the family with him?"

"Looks like somebody is," Grampy would say, and Grand would say, "Sherry, go bring me up about six more potatoes from the cellar, and another jar of green beans.

The lady of the visiting family was greeted with a hug, she never sat down, and instead, would say, "Mabel, I'll peel these taters for you if you got another knife."

Grand would hand her the knife, and a clean, starched apron, and so it went, as if nothing unusual was happening.

Sometimes they'd stay until mid-afternoon, visiting, catching up on all of the local news and gossip, while the kids, if they had any, were playing outside in the yard.

They didn't have any toys to play with. They didn't sit around huffing and puffing because they were bored.

They were climbing trees, and playing chase, and hide and go seek, and running like wild puppies turned loose.

That way of life is gone.

Today, you need an invitation to visit, or you have to call and ask if they're going to be home, that you need to bring something by that they'd asked for. And you don't stay and visit. Neither one of you feel like you have the time, and have too many other things pending.

And so the connection between people is reduced to acquaintances, and the female bond is sometimes non-existent, because you're both vying for the same job, or your kids don't like each other.

And the kids, if they are along, don't know the meaning of entertaining themselves. Half of them talk back to their parents and demand this and expect that.

And the other half are left to their own devices.

I'm not being critical of either lifestyle.

What I'm saying is that....I have lived/am living both worlds.

It's not that I'm old fashioned. It's simply a fact that having experienced both lifestyles, and lived through the evolution that took them from then to now, I can truthfully say that something precious has been lost in the process.

Women used to trust each other. They took care of each other. They were at the births of each other's babies. They helped other women lay out, and bury their husbands. They shared food. They shared both sorrows, and small joys, and were sincerely glad to see each other. Men worked. Children came and went and grew up and left. But it was the woman who was the hub of each family. She loved. She sheltered. She fed the hungry and rocked the sick babies. And no one else knew or understood the isolation of that time. The only people who could speak to her world, and understand what hurt her...were other women.

My sisters...don't forget yourselves in the midst of the many ways life pulls you.

Don't waste time and energy stressing about adding one more thing to your life, just because you want it on a resume.

Give your kids responsibilities first. Technology second.

Teach them that you matter, by not allowing people to speak rudely to you, and don't allow them to do it, either.

Life isn't about what you have, or what you did, or where you went on vacation.

Life is a gift.

Don't forget that love comes with it, and stays with you, long after you've opened the package and tossed away the bows.

$$\approx$$

The eighteen hours of pain finally passed around 7:00 a.m. yesterday morning. I slept through Denise cleaning my house. Only three or four times since she began here, have I told her to just clean around me, and that I couldn't make myself move. :)

She's the feet and hands I always need...she's my sweet, sweet friend. She and Ash move at about the same speed...High and fast. LOL

I think I heard the vacuum once.

I drank enough vinegar during the flare, that I made myself nauseous, but as always...it by gosh works.

I pretend I'm pouring myself a shot...add a splash of cold water and down it goes. Chase it with more cold water or you'll lose your breath.

And just FYI...vinegar is fabulous for a lot of health modalities.

Thank you, my Bobby...you always kept me on the right paths.

No matter what I am doing around the house, first thing each morning I'm listening to WholeTones. That's a compilation of different melodies, like different songs. It's just beautiful music, but in the background of each piece, there is one continuing note...you aren't really aware of it, unless you listen for it...but the notes are each at a different vibration of energy. My choice is always the one at 528 HZ...the vibration of love....the energy vibration of GAIA....our earth. And if I get a little stressed or feel myself starting to lose a little pep, I just sit down, close my eyes, and play it again. It's only a couple of seconds over 22 minutes long. Each CD in that collection is the exact same length...just at different vibrations.

I don't own an iPod. I can't stand ear buds in my ears...I don't want to be hooked up to technology to hear it. I want it in the room, filling the house...or in the car...filling up the space.

It's also available on YouTube.

Oh wow... I just surprised myself. You see what happened? Without consciously doing it, I gave you a solution for a specific pain, and a solution for lifting you up.

Thanks, Spirit. None of this is intentional. I only just realized it as I read it back.... So...I guess these are your messages for today.

The life you live is the way you will be remembered.

Not what you're dreaming about...not how you WANT your life to be. Just the way you are. The way you move through each day.

Like footprints in the mud...you are leaving a very distinct path.

So think about that...every time you make a decision, every time you throw a public fit, every time you react in anger, every time you belittle...throw negativity of any kind out into the Universe...

You leave that indelible imprint of who you are.

ॐ

Got a message from Scout yesterday. He wanted us to get some to-go food and have lunch with his Mama before actual classes begin. Of course, I said yes. Sounded like a great plan. I asked him where wanted to get food, and he messaged back, Johnny's. It's famous for its burgers and onion rings.. So I pick him up, we order, and as we're sitting there waiting for them to bring it to the car (they have carhop service, as well as dine-in) I said, I'm glad you picked this place. I love their black bean burgers. And he nodded, and then it hit me. I said, "You picked it BECAUSE of me, didn't you? Because it has food that I can eat." He just looked at me, grinned a little, and said, "yeah."

I swear...he has THE biggest heart. I don't know very many almost 17 year old boys who even think about stuff like that. I just bragged on him to Kathy this morning. I could hear the pride and the love in her voice when she said, "yeah, I'll keep him."

He is a quiet, peace-loving old soul, and we are blessed he belongs to us.

It is a freeing thing to know that you are accepted as you are.

That you are loved without boundaries.

My path in this life was not about having my heart and soul rejected, which some children experience. I was surrounded in love. Knowing that way of life was crucial to being able to empathize. So that when the empath in me sensed the sorrow or rage in someone else, that I would understand they were not acting out because they were bad...but because they suffered from a lack of love.

We all see life through the eyes of our own experiences.

This is why misunderstandings often occur. We see a truth through what we know...and we only know how we have lived.

You can never judge, or speak for someone else, because their life experiences are not yours. You don't know what they've seen, what they've endured, what horrors have shaped their existence.

YOU DON'T KNOW.

When you were in school, and the teacher asked someone for an answer....did you raise your hand, even though you had no idea what the answer was?

Of course not. You sat in total silence and scooted down in your seat, praying she wouldn't point at you.

And yet....as adults...we believe we don't have to know the answer to get loud about it.

We just want to be heard.

It is everyone's right to be heard when they have suffered injustice, or grief.

Yet again...like the child in class...if you don't have an answer for the problem, the kindest, wisest thing you can do is show love.

❦

Today was hairdo day. And lunch at Panera Bread (tomato soup and an oatmeal cookie). Then a flying trip to Walmart, then my counseling session with Leslie Draper. I'm home, feet up, and there may be a brief nap in my future.

It is the light within people that attracts us to them--like moths to a flame.

We don't know that's what it is. All we know is we feel safe in their presence, and they make us feel good about ourselves, and when we leave them, we are happy, feeling satisfied...feeling blessed.

And within that same rule of thumb, we have people we dread going to see. It's not easy to be in their presence, and we spend our time with them in constant apology for nothing we did, or a building anger that we don't understand.

It's their vibe...their negativity. It's the energy they emanate, which comes from the dissatisfaction of their lives, or rage at the injustices they have suffered.

It's hard to walk that fine line between the empathy you feel for them, and the knowledge that you will suffocate if you don't get away.

You can't fix them.

You're not even supposed to try.

We each have to come to our own realizations that there are things in our lives that we need to change.

You can hear it daily from a spouse. You can hear it daily from a friend, or from a pastor. But you never recognize yourself in those messages because you don't realize that's who you are...that's what you've become.

Our paths are to always be kind.

And just keep them in our prayers.

꧁

Too many of my FB friends are having troubles today, and I cannot do anything for any of them to change it, other than send love and pray.

So...me being me...I am in the kitchen.

The custard I made for my ice cream machine has finally cooled enough to use. I'm going to try out my new ice cream maker.

I've had it a while, but didn't take the time to make the custard to go in it.

You have to cook it, then let it cool at least two hours...and all the--work then wait--business isn't necessarily relaxing.

But today called for desperate measures, so I decided time WAS needed today to get calm and refocus.

I'll let you know later if I did the ice cream right.

Never used one of these things before.

I grew up with hand cranked, crushed ice. and ice cream salt makers, and Mother never cooked a custard. She used whole milk plus some cream, sugar, vanilla, and Rennet Tablets in her recipe.

I have an electric ice cream freezer that's at least 20 years old, but it's also crushed ice and ice cream salt process.

This baby is a--freeze the bowl that the custard goes in--cook and cool the custard--pour in the machine and push a couple of buttons--process.

Today...it doesn't really matter whether it's a huge success or not. I just had to stay busy.

And I keep telling myself... 'this, too, shall pass.'

I keep reminding myself that other people's troubles are not my business to fix. They are happening in their lives not mine.

I have lots of things that happen beneath my roof that I don't talk about, and some I do... but I never expect anyone to solve my problems for me.

I accept there is a lesson in it, or it wouldn't be happening.

Even when I hate it with all my heart...or even when I was so worried I couldn't sleep...not even when I love people I loved, did I ever expect answers from others. It was happening in my life...on my path.

Sometimes I would get an answer to something from someone else who already knew what to do...but I don't ever expect solutions.

Staying out of other people's emotional upheavals is probably that hardest thing there is about being an empath. We try so hard not to lock into emotions that don't belong to us, but sometimes we're not sure whether what we're feeling belongs to us, or to someone else. And when you know the people in trouble or in pain, it's even harder.

So God love all of you in crisis today.

You know who you are. And if you're in the neighborhood,

I have ice cream.

&.

Every emotion we feel has its own palette of colors or sounds.

Tears color grief, joy, and fear.

The flush on our face can go from a delicate pink of embarrassment, to a dark, angry red.

When laughter is emanating joy, it flows easily, peppered with higher pitched tones, like the trill of a songbird.

Lower the pitch of laughter to color derision, and the sharp, barking sounds of an angry dog can be heard among the tones.

In the cry for help, the color of fear is always high-pitched, and the notes held for as long as the person draws breath.

On our knees before God, our emotions waver between the quiet sounds of thanksgiving, to a whisper for intercession, or the screaming rage of disbelief.

But with any or every emotion, the presence of tears is universal.

They heal. They cleanse. They release. And in the last few breaths we take, they become the ending seal of who we were, as we leave this Earth for home.

When tears fall, there is nothing to hide. No shame to feel.

They're just the strokes of God's paintbrush upon the canvasses of our lives

&.

I finished the copy edits for *Dark Water Rising* and sent it back to my editor at Mira, checking another job off of my to-do list.

Today was for silence.

I came home after Love Church, ate my lunch and then turned off the noise. I needed quiet today. Some days more so than others.

Being in my house with the television off, no music, no people talking, no animals in my house needing my attention.

Just me.

So I could listen for the messages.

I sat, closed my eyes, and began to focus on the sounds of my own breath. And then my heartbeat. Even my house fell silent, as if sensing that creaks and pops were not welcome at that time.

Noise blocks our senses.

We can't heed our own inner warning systems when we are surrounded by the cacophony that comes with city living.

Too many people, and too much noise is overwhelming.

I long for the quiet I used to have out on the ranch with Bobby. Sitting out on the back porch watching a herd of deer come out of the woods to graze in the back pasture with the horses.

Watching a flock of turkeys moving along the edge of the trees. Hearing the first yips of the coyotes as they emerge from their dens for night hunting.

Seeing the big barn owl lift off from a tree in the back yard and fly away into a dusky sky.

There we sat, with the dogs at his feet and a cat in his lap. If there was an animal in sight, it went straight to him.

A little quail would call from the woods, and soon the mate would call back.

When it called the second time, I called back with a whistle that sounded like their call. And as it answered, Bobby would grin.

"You are a good Indian," he would say. "Your call fooled the bird."

"I don't know what I said to him, but I hope he doesn't hold me to it," I would say, which made him laugh even more.

Two souls.

One heart.

Beating in rhythm.

And so it is.

§▲

Denise was here.

My house is shiny clean and smells like Pine-Sol. Wheee.

You don't need to be alone to find peace.

You don't have to be on your knees to talk to God.

You don't need a clean house before you can rest.

When the body needs rest, you feel it.

When your spirit needs rest, you can't think.

When your heart is being pulled in too many directions by people you love, wanting more, more, more from you, you're the one who will break.

How many times do you have to hear the words..."You can't love another until you first love you."

You can't help someone else, if there's not enough of you left to help yourself.

Life does not have to be perfect to find peace, or joy, or happiness. All of those are inner emotions, coming from an acceptance of where YOU are, at this moment, in the world.

If you are sick, in a hospital, and in pain...then take courage in the fact that you are where you need to be to get help.

If you have chosen to stay in a bad situation, for reasons known only to you, then accept that you are where you are by choice, and make peace with it.

Nothing good ever comes from living with regret. You have the option to change, or if you can't make a decision, then you have chosen to stay where you are, doing what you always do.

God isn't going to intercede in your free will.

You keep blasting through life making one bad move after another and then throw your hands up and pray, God save me! then you get mad when He doesn't. And you blame Him for your situation...or you blame everyone else.

It's so easy to pass blame.

Poor choices, poor health, poor relationships, poor attitudes...and you have the perfect storm ongoing in your life.

If you don't like it, then just stop doing the same things.

That road doesn't have a beginning or an end.

It's a constant loop that plays over and over in your life

until you either step out of it, or you simply stay until you die.

It's all up to you.

෫෯

This is going to seem like an impossible or improbable request to many, but it will matter greatly to all of you in the coming days. So hear me out, and if you don't agree or don't like it, please do me the courtesy of just moving along.

This message is for the people who are ready to hear it.

For every crisis, for every troubling news report, for every injustice and crime happening, people hear about it, or read about it, and panic. Even when it doesn't directly affect them, many are unable to detach enough from the fear and tragedies that they are making themselves sick. Making THEMSELVES sick. They fight over different viewpoints, which translates to being in a constant state of anger and unrest, which then affects their homes, their jobs, their families, and ultimately, their health and well-being.

It is vastly important during this time of unrest, that you find a way to let go of that which you cannot change, and find a place of peace within you. And the easiest way to do that, is counteract the ugliness in the world with good. Doing good. Being good. Loving. Loving those around you, and loving your fellow man.

The more things you do for others from the goodness of your heart, the more you will be protected from the trauma of someone else's stress. It fills you up so completely, that there is truly no room for hate to come in.

For every person who 'wakes up' to this reality, the more their own light will grow. And the brighter their lights, the better their lives, and the lives of others around them will become.

You can't change lives, unless you first change yourself.

Everyone talks about making changes...that they need change...they want change.

But nothing changes until people change.

We have been at war somewhere on this planet during every generation since man first set foot here. If it was the answer, it would have already worked. All it did was create more animosity between people.

Step away from wanting a life with power, and seek a simpler life....one with enough. Not more. Just enough.

Have a love for humanity within you. Not just for the people you know.

The happier/more satisfied you are, the brighter your inner light becomes, and the brighter your light, the more wonderful are the things that come to you.

If you are someone who begrudges the good news of others.

If you are someone who is envious of people with bigger houses and fancier cars.

If you think your happiness hinges on the amount of money you have, or the popular friends you have in your circle, then you are living a life of constant negativity.

For every dark, selfish, hateful thing you think or say, you are instantly...and universally, linked with others all over the world who are thinking the same way.

You might not have meant to, but you just tuned into the frequency and raised the antennae of your soul to pull in darkness, the likes of which you cannot imagine.

You have the option to change the way you think and live.

Let go of hate.

Choose you.

Choose light.

Choose love.

໖

I'm sitting in the quiet of my home, with the scent of toasted left-over biscuit and a fried egg still lingering--a remnant of my supper, and hearing a siren somewhere in the distance, and thinking to myself how blessed I am to be here.

I've lived through two wrecks, both of which should have killed me, and a surgery from which I would not wake up.

I've watched two of the people closest to me take their last breaths.

I have love for the life I live, but I have absolutely no fear of dying.

I never thought about living the last years of my life alone, and yet here I am, with no regrets.

Accepting your path and following it faithfully isn't easy, but we didn't come here for easy.

We came here to learn, and I have learned many things.

I think, if I had to pick one lesson out of a lifetime of hard-lessons learned, it would be this:

I'd rather be alone, than along for someone else's ride.

🍂

Some days I just know what I know.

I woke up this morning, looked up at the ceiling and thought, today the sewing machine repairman is gonna be here...in my bedroom...this afternoon. And I frowned. I am uncomfortable with repairmen of any kind in my house, especially if I don't know them. So I get up and start preparing to block him out of as much of my world as I can, while still letting him get to the machine.

The first thing I did was shut the doors to my bathroom.

I already knew...(don't ask.. I just know what I know)... that he would call and ask if he could come here early, and then once he got in my house, THE FIRST THING he would ask was if he could use my bathroom.

So I went straight to the guest bathroom in the hall and made sure everything was in order then went about my business, reminding myself that whatever vibe I got off of him, I would be smudging away as soon as he left.

He was due to come at 1:00 p.m.

He called me at 12:30 and asked if he could come early.

I said yes, I was home, and three minutes later he's at my door.

I walked him back to my bedroom, he went to the machine and sat down, then got up, looked straight at the closed doors leading into my bathroom and asked if he could use my bathroom, that he just had lunch with his daughter, yadayada. (and I'm thinking...they don't have bathrooms where you ate?). I pointed to the hall. "Follow me," and led him to the guest bathroom.

And I'm sitting in my office thinking...some days, I just know what I know.

When he went back into my room I went with him, and as he sat down, I saw him notice the ceremonial tomahawk beside my bed that was made from the jawbone of a deer. He glanced back at me, a little startled. I just smiled, and stood there. He worked on it for a bit, but it was still slipping, and when he said he needed to take it to his shop to clean because the oil had settled and was gunky, I knew that was the truth. As soon as he left, I smudged my whole house.

He's gone, and now so is his energy.

Between me and my guardians we've got this.

&

I have discovered the secret to a good night's rest.

Don't freakin' go to bed at 2:00 a.m. Sharon Kay!

I went to bed at 10:00 p.m. last night and woke up at 7:30 this morning, in a good mood and well rested.

Why didn't I try this sooner?

Charlie Hunam look-alike, aka Colt, is mowing my yard.

And it's trash day.

And I need to do laundry.

And none of that is a problem. It's just what's happening.

And there is no one cracking a whip telling me what to do, or what I need to be doing.

I leave lights on when I want to.

I adjust the temperature in my house to suit myself.

I eat when I want to.

I sleep when I want to.

I lived by a clock and other people's rules and deadlines for 2/3 of my life.

I have earned my right to be my own boss.

And the best part of that is that I surround myself with people who don't push my buttons.

At this age, I'm just tired enough of humans who believe they are beyond reproach, that I will push back.

#toomanylifetimesundermybelt
#nopatienceforfools
#whiningdoesnotbecomeyou
The light within us burns eternal.

In the darkest night, on the farthest hill, in a crashing storm, in our greatest grief, the light of just one bright soul can lead us to grace. To safety. All the way home.

❧

The saddest thing about growing old, is people who don't know how to accept it.

They spend time and money trying to regain their youth, or at least the perception of it, and never experience what it means to be present in their own bodies.

If you spent your life chasing love and never learned to love yourself, then you missed the lesson.

We didn't come here to be worshiped.

We came here with the intent of loving and accepting one another.

There is a kind of grace in the slower steps and stooping shoulders...a bowing down to the inevitable weight time.

Hair does not lose color as it ages.

It changes into the heavenly color of starlight.

As your sight grows dimmer, your soul light grows brighter to make up for the loss.

When sad things happen, and hard times come, you have the comfort in knowing the truth of..'this, too, shall pass,' because you've already lived it again and again.

And if you've embraced the real you, then you have long since moved past caring what other people think about you, and don't intend to waste your time judging them.

One of the best parts of getting older.....A part of you is beginning to remember home.

Every scar on our bodies, every line in our brows is proof that we survived.

We didn't run from life...we faced it and walked through it.

We stayed the course.
We fought the fight.
We don't want new.
We want durable.
We don't need things.
All we need is a place to be.
And Love.

ॐ

There once was a woman who grew thirsty, and went to the well to get herself a drink. But as she leaned over to dip out the water, she saw her reflection and stopped, mesmerized by how the sun formed a halo around her head, and how beautiful the shape of her face appeared.

Another woman approached, and she, too, leaned over to get a drink. The first woman watched...and saw that woman's reflection and felt envy. She was prettier and younger. So the first woman ran home, intent on fixing her hair a different way, and putting lotions on her face to smooth her skin. Then she put on her prettiest dress and went back to the well, and was pleased at what she saw.

And then a third woman approached, and the first woman watched her lean over to dip her cup into the water, and again, she was struck dumb with envy. That woman's hair was the color of sunlight, and her eyes, the color of the sky. So the first woman ran home again, and repeated her rituals, and changed her clothes, and fixed her hair, and went back...then repeated the process again and again and again...until the sun was going down, and she could no longer see her own reflection.

She was so certain that this time she would be perfect, that she stood at the well all night, waiting for sunrise.

The people found her there the next morning, lying against the well, with the cup in her hand.

"How sad," they said. "She was such a kind woman. She was the best neighbor...the best friend anyone could want. Look! There's the cup in her hand...all she must have needed was water. How sad. How sad."

It's not about how you look.

It's about the path you walk in the world.

Don't get lost in the drama around you

When all you needed was a drink from the well.

~

Sky above.

Earth below.

Oceans wide.

Air doth flow.

When the balance of nature is immeasurably broken,

And humanity has failed to address it,

the gift of living here will be taken away.

You can't own what was never for sale, and yet man defied the balance of human nature and took it. And from that moment on, has been fighting for ownership ever since.

Lightworkers used to stand quiet in the background of existence, doing what they do in the name of Love, good, and mercy, to keep the balance of humanity in check, but that time is gone.

The balance of humanity as we knew it is forever broken.

Lightworkers saw it happening hundreds of years before..and began stepping out and stepping up, and dying for it...doing what they must to speak up before it's too late.

People think shouting and marching and fighting and killing will stop the darkness...but darkness feeds on discord...on marching in anger, on shouting in rage, on killing in cold blood.

Even though they mean well, the dark side feeds on their behavior.

All of you know there is only one way to push back the night...and that's to turn on the light--the lights around you, and the lights within you.

Lightworkers now have become warriors.

Warriors of all ages and races.

You know our names.

You know our faces.

We don't hide. We don't deny.

Where many gather in the name of the great I AM, so grows the light until it is one massive, blinding, LOVE-filled, living thing of such power, that the darkness cannot fight.

When there are no shadows...there is no place for darkness to hide.

In the name of God, show Love to someone today.

In the name of Love, be kind in all ways.

Do it in YOUR name.

Do it FOR God.

Do it for all of us.

Before it's too late.

xw

Today has been a day of peace for me. My son, Chris, came around noon, and then my daughter, Kathy, and family came shortly afterward. We ate homemade ice cream and fresh sliced strawberries as promised, and just like I knew he would, Chris had two bowls before he stopped. :)

I got the okay from Mira (publisher) on the proposal I submitted for my next book. I'm really excited to do this. I proposed it as a possible series, so not sure if they want the one...or if a series works for them, too. It has more mystery than suspense, and two great lead characters who would be recurring in every subsequent book. We'll see how it goes.

Life is so complicated.

Even at the best of times, we are impacted by the pain and trouble of people we love. When that happens, our knee jerk reaction is to get in the middle of it. To try and fix it, or even worse, take sides, which does nothing positive for situations.

When children are involved, the rules are different...sometimes someone needs to step in, but once children are grown, you are not meant to interfere, or keep fixing their messes. When you do that, they never see the error of their ways. They don't learn from the mistakes, because you keep fixing them.

Even when it's your own children grown....you have to remember that they are now on their own path, and must make their own choices., and learn the lessons they need to learn.

You have to allow them the same freedom of choice that you have. Think how you'd feel if the people in your family started telling YOU how to live, and what to do and not do.

Like what happens when parents and grandparents age...and family starts stepping in and telling them they can no longer drive, and it's not safe for them to live alone.

They don't like it one bit, and sometimes don't understand it.

But when people are competent adults, we have to give them the same respect.

Nobody said you had to approve.

Nobody said you have to like it.

But it's not your place to interfere.

It's life.

And it's hard.

And beautiful.

And precious.

And it's yours.

ॐ

Making homemade vanilla ice cream for tomorrow with fresh sliced strawberries on the side for when my son stops by. Kathy and family are off work tomorrow, so they will be in on it.

Of all the desserts my son loves to eat...homemade ice cream and berry cobbler top the list. I used Ree Drummond's recipe, because she makes enough that she has to freeze it in two separate batches...so knowing Chris, Kathy, Scout, Ash, and Moi will be having some, I thought I'd best do the wholeything. My son has never stopped at one bowl if he could help it. <3

Made me wish for Bobby to be here. He would be so in love with this Cuisinart ice cream freezer, he'd be wanting ice cream every day... <3

It sure beats being the weight on top of the old-time crank freezers, which was what Diane and I were when Daddy made ice cream. He'd pack the old wooden bucket full of ice and ice cream salt, then put the crank on and top it with a folded up gunny sack. I usually wound up being first, because I wanted to eat ice chips. I wasn't even bothered by the salt crystal on them, I just wiped them off and popped it in my mouth.

Every time Daddy needed to add more ice and salt, I had to get up, then back down went the gunny sack, and back down I sat, listening to the stories all of the adults were telling, and watching the way Daddy's blue eyes would dance while he was telling one. He was an amazing storyteller, and always had a rapt audience.

After a while, my butt was pretty much frozen, and I was starting to complain, so he'd yell at Diane, and she'd come running, her face beet-red from playing, and happy to sit down on something cool.

Life was simple for kids, but adults had the same worries they have now, we just never knew it. Mother and Daddy didn't believe in telling kids when something was wrong, or when money was tight. And since we never expected treats to begin with, we didn't notice the differences in what they were buying at the store. God knows we never went hungry. Mother canned and froze everything in sight until it was down to dry stalks, and she was an amazing cook and even better at managing money, which was good, because Daddy was not. <3

So today, I'm in a happy place, remembering the good times with family, and the love in which we were raised.

Not everyone will have the same life experiences, but it does not mean that they haven't suffered great heartache and loss. Life is all about the lessons learned.

If you didn't grow up in love, then you need to love yourself.

꙳

There's more unseen between earth and sky than some will ever know...or believe.

And that's okay, but the constant presence of your angels, spirits, and your guides is real, and it's so easy to understand when you understand how loved our souls are, how precious we are to the great I Am, and how beloved we are by the Universe as a whole. We are part of the God-light.

The Cherokee believe if there is but one drop of Cherokee blood in you, then you are still part of the whole, and so you are viewed as belonging.

So it is with God. We are all part of Him, therefore our soul connection to every other living soul on Earth is a given.

For this reason alone, the discord we have among us is not how God meant us to be. We knew before we came here how to access everything we needed to live out this human life. But unfortunately, that memory is erased once we are here. Some souls quickly find their way back to manifesting. Some never even know that it's a thing they can do until they've lived out this life and gone home. But there are some souls among us, who still have a hot-line to angels, who can see and talk to spirit, and they become the bridge between us as humans, and home.

The simple knowing that exists...that it's even possible to learn what we've forgotten...makes the understanding of WHY so important, when we suffer so many heartaches and disappointments. It's why we came--to grow our empathy and light, to grow our understanding and forgiveness.

It is our truth of lessons learned.

At all times, they are with us, slowing us down so we don't run a red light, delaying us in ways to keep us from being in accidents, whispering to us when we sleep to remind us we are never alone.

They are the breath of wind against your face.

The sudden shiver you feel for no reason.

The glimpse of sunlight that you needed on a dark and cloudy day.

And often the miracle you didn't even know you needed.

&

When I was little, every day was a new day for adventures for me. I knew Mother would make something good for our breakfast. Weather permitting, Diane and I would be outside playing until she called us in for dinner. Running in and out of the house during the day didn't happen much. We didn't have air conditioning or fans, so it was actually cooler outside beneath a shade tree than inside. And in the winter, we'd play out until we froze out, and then run back inside and race to the old potbelly stove to get warm. When I started school, we moved from the house by the creek to a rent house in the country south of Paden. The house was old with unfinished hardwood floors and walls with no insulation. I think there were gas stoves that we would back up to, to get warm, but they didn't heat even half of a room, let alone the house, and yet the discomfort is not what I think of from that time. It was family.

My world WAS my family. And school broadened my horizons greatly. Walking the quarter mile road from our house to the road to catch the bus. Meeting new kids to play with, when I'd only before played with my sister and cousins. Being so quiet in the room because the teacher said, 'be quiet', to all of us, and it never occurred to me not to mind her.

Thanks to my mother, I already knew how to read before I started school, so it made everything else easier to learn.

But I am an introvert...and at that age, painfully so. Mostly, I went through my day, doing what I was told, and waiting for the time when that big yellow school bus would come take me home.

Because....family was where I could be me. Not afraid. Secure in the knowledge that I was safe.

That was many years ago, and much about my life has changed...but the inner me is still my true North.

I'm most comfortable in my home...with the people I love coming and going through my days.

I've reached the age where there's nothing more I want in life than to be safe and comfortable...and yet, more is still asked of me. I am on my path...I know my truth...I haven't finished what I came here to do.

Today is another day for me.

Today is also another day for you.

Do you know your path?

Are you living a joy-filled life?

If you're not, it is an easy thing to do.

All you have to do is wake up with the knowledge that every day is a new day for YOU. You have the opportunity to change. You have the opportunity to grow. You have the opportunity to be happy.

It doesn't cost money. It doesn't take time.

It's just you, changing the way you think and feel.

Today...

ॐ

I watched the movie LION for the first time last night. Sobbed off and on all the way through it. Most tragic, heart-breaking, uplifting and positive ending movie I've seen in years...and it was based on a true story.

It was even hard to fall asleep later, because the images in that film were so dire, it has forever altered my perception of poverty.

I'm still thinking about it this morning, knowing this exists today, just as it has existed there for centuries.

It's not a judgement at all against the way life is there, because I always knew the caste system existed in that part of the world, and I was very aware of the vast numbers of people who existed in such a small part of the world, which only adds to the poverty level.

But last night, I saw it through the eyes of a child, and then as a man grown, and I will never forget it...or get over it.

I could never, never visit there. As an empath, it would kill me.

I just....

There are no words.

That little face.

He was so lost.

I will never again...even jokingly say, I don't know what I want to eat. The fact that I have choices is more than enough for which to be grateful.

The fact that I have a bed and shelter.

And I know where I am and who loves me.

I also know there are children here in similar situations.

Tragedy is not pertinent to only one part of the world.

But LION put a face on it for me.

As hard as it was to watch, I knew all the way through it that I was supposed to see it.

Only when you have been shown contrasts, can you see where you really are in the world.

I saw my continuing path there.

Just like the child who needed to find home to heal.

So do we all...live this life as it unfolds, so that we, too, can go home to heal what being human did to us.

❧

Each day is a gift.

We unwrap it every morning when we get out of bed.

Some days we love the gift. It's just what we hoped for.

Other days, we would give anything to be able to return it.

But that would be rude...a gift given was done with thought and love, just as each day we are still here.

We have an option to receive the gift with gratitude and grace, or we can be ungrateful and resent the burden that may come with the day.

Often, we focus on all the wrong things.

You wanted a sunny day and it is raining.

You wanted a day off, and got called in to work because of an emergency.

You woke up sick, and have a job with no leeway for illness.

You either show up or you're fired.

There are all kinds of scenarios about your day, and when they are hard days, you almost always feel the full weight of the burden.

When they are good days, you are happy and fly through your work.

What you have to realize is that you're not the only one who feels this way, but some of the people you work with have learned to leave separate their lives in such a way that they do not bring personal troubles to work, and do not take professional problems home.

The trick is the moment you start feeling angst or anger, just stop. Remind yourself that you are in control of your own emotions. Whatever is happening is just another thing in your day. It's not the end of the world, and it can't ruin your day unless you let it.

Be the first person to shift the negative focus to positive.

If a flower can grow and blossom between the cracks in a sidewalk, then you can surely find a way to blossom within the hours of your day.

❧

Comparing a person who has never experienced racial injustice, to a person who's whole life has been littered with it, is ridiculous.

If you don't see the holes in your argument, then there's nothing else to be said.

You do you.

Just know the whole point you think you're making doesn't work, because there IS NO comparison.

Not a subject for discussion.

Merely an observation in the flaw of humanity.

❧

Fear is nothing more than an unknown.

If you knew what was ahead of you, you might regret, you might get anxious, you could prepare for the battle you see coming, or you might sigh with relief.

If you weren't afraid, you might not feel the need to separate yourself from people you don't understand.

If you weren't afraid, you would realize different isn't wrong.

If you weren't afraid, you could face whatever life just dropped in your lap, without an emotional breakdown.

If you weren't afraid, you're first instinct would not be to deny, or rage, or fight.

If there were no unknowns in this life, we wouldn't be here.

We come here to learn. So if there were no surprises, no lessons to learn, no trouble to get through, no tragedies to survive, no grief to feel, we would all still be in spirit.

So what is the answer?

Love.

Love is the answer.

If you acted out of love, rather than fear or ignorance, think of the difference you would make.

A misunderstanding would be solved with a hug or a laugh.

Unexpected trouble would be dealt with calmly, knowing that whatever the outcome, God has your back.

When you try to control what's going on in your life, you only make things more complicated.

Life is happening as a lesson, and the lesson is never about controlling the outcome, anymore than buying a lottery ticket is, and expecting to win, assuming money would solve all your problems.

Life lessons are like pop quizzes in school.

You never know when you're going to get one.

But the solution is just always be prepared.

If you studied your lessons in class, you usually managed a pop quiz quite well.

But if you had been focused on other things all through the year, and were just skimming through the class to get by, you will most certainly fail the test.

So it is with life.

When you practice tolerance and kindness, and have understanding and love in your heart, you will have a greater grasp of what you are capable of doing, to get through the life altering event you suddenly experience.

I am a Lightworker.

I stand in the light.

I am not afraid.

If you don't know how to grow your light,

Practice kindness.

Practice love.

§♭

Today: I have asked God

To send the white healing light of the Holy Spirit to you if you are in pain.

To send strength for you if you are in distress.

To send His peace and grace to you, if you are in a state of grief.

To send light and joy to you, if you are suffering depression.

I pray this for all of you every night, but today, I felt led to ask it of Him today as well.

There is much turmoil in the world right now.

Part of it is people led.

Part of it is energetically caused.

Part of it is weather related.

We are all made of the same thing—particles of energy.

And we are all filled with the same thing--pieces of light from the great I AM.

We all react to outer stimuli.

But because of the human lives we have lived, we react in different ways and each have different purposes.

Know that I pray LOVE.

Know that I PRAY love.

Know THAT I pray love.

KNOW that I pray love.

Understand the wording:

I didn't send it specifically to anyone...

I sent it into the Universe.

Remember...that which you speak will come back to you a thousand fold.

Understand that I have prayed aloud for LOVE, so that as it returns, it comes to all.

LOVE IS LIGHT.

LIGHT IS LOVE.

Be at peace in your hearts, for you are loved.

ਔ

I am making homemade chocolate ice cream. I do love ice cream and not supposed to be eating carbs, but what the heck. Today I needed to do something besides write or think about writing.

It will be done in about ten minutes or so, and I'll scoop it out and put it in the freezer to get hard. Kathy will come get some later.

Yard guy mowed this morning.

I haven't left the house except to get the mail and my paper out of the driveway.

This is one of those huddle-up days for me—when quiet is my friend.

I listened to a solid hour of music for healing inflammation like what I get from RA. I've been doing this daily for a week. There are lots of modalities to choose from on YouTube, but I chose the Rife one for inflammation. All I know is, my left foot is barely swollen and the pain is minimal compared to last week. I refused the prescription medicine for RA over a year ago. It ticked off my RA specialist and we haven't seen each other since. She named off the things that could happen to me if RA was left untreated...and I named off the side effects of any of the meds she would prescribe to treat it. I won.

It was my choice, and I made it, just like I chose to quit meat rather than take a prescription med for gout, which also has side effects I don't want to deal with.

I'll choose my way to live and so it is.

Since I have been productive today in some way other than sitting on my butt and typing, I feel more kindly toward working tonight. LOL

Lots of good things happening related to writing. Agent called today telling me money came in on the last Blessings book I turned in, and she was contacted by a publisher telling me they would happily publish me anytime I was ready to make a deal.

It's news like this that keeps writers hopeful and working...knowing they are valued in this way.

I have a pretty rigid work schedule into part of next year, but there will be time for new deals. I'll make sure of it.

Never pass up a positive opportunity.

Do something for yourself.

Something that makes you happy.

It's the best medicine you'll ever take.

⚜

I take each day as it comes without expectations, grateful for whatever is put in my path.

So far, today has been a total blessing.

I went to LOVE Church this morning.

Had lunch with Kathy and Ash afterward. She made everything special that I could eat and it was wonderful. I had a big tossed salad with sweet peppers and red onion from their garden. Then she made THE BEST vegan wild rice and veggie soup, and we had hot biscuits and honey to go with it.

Ash showed me a jar of the green tomato relish they made. This is the batch that accidentally got a triple helping of Jalapeno peppers to go with the California Reapers (super hot) that were already in it. It's a funny story and an accident that many Jalapeno peppers wound up in there. He'd chopped so many vegetables and peppers that day that were meant to go in the relish, that he sort of lost track of what he was doing when he began chopping up a bunch of the Jalapeno peppers to put in the freezer. Without thinking, he just dumped them in the relish, too, and didn't realize what he'd done until later that night, when Kathy said he suddenly jumped up from the sofa and said, "OH SHIT! I put all those Jalapeno peppers in the relish that I was chopping up to freeze."

They could only laugh because it was too late to fix it. So this the Oh Shit relish that got canned. LOLOLOL

I also came home with two meals worth of the wild-rice soup when I left, and when I got home, found this beautiful bouquet that Ash had sneaked over and left for me while I was at church.

Scout came home from a weekend Boy Scout camp-out, so I got to see him before I left.

I am blessed today in every way...I had fun, good food and shared a lot of laughter with people I love.

Nothing can beat that for me.

I know this much is true:

Bad news won't take you down.

It's how you receive it that makes the difference.

§.

So...I can't believe how many people began their day with a negative post today, but God bless you.

All I know is, beginning the day with a "I dare you to disagree with me" post is like getting out of the car and stepping into a mud puddle. You've already begun the day on the wrong foot.

I punched myself in the nose this morning. Actually the bridge of my nose...right where my glasses rest. I was yanking on the comforter trying to make my bed, my hand slipped off and I hit myself in the nose. Whack!. Jesus walked on Water, but did that ever hurt! And then I started laughing. I mean...who does that?

I already have a little skinned up place and the beginnings of a small bruise. But I laughed instead of having a Smith cussing fit. And for all the Smiths who are kin to me who read this, they'll know exactly what I mean. :)

I gave all that up years ago when I figured out all it did was make me madder...and no one else cared how mad I got, which makes it worse. LOLOLOL

Denise is here cleaning. We laughed about me punching myself. She gets me. Laughter is key in my day, and even if it was at my own expense today, it was a good way to begin the day.

If you want to be happier in life, the first thing you have to do is love yourself.

You can't find love, if you don't love yourself.

You can't be truly happy, if all you do is resent others, and want what you don't have.

Things aren't important.

People are.

When you let them down, you're betraying yourself, as well.

If you promise something to someone,

Keep your word.

If you don't want to do something other people are doing, then don't.

Going along to make other people happy only makes you resentful, and then what have you gained?

Nothing but more built-in resentment.

You think you're mad at people,

But you're really just mad at yourself.

Next time, just say, no.

Next time, just be you.

❦

Every time I read a sweet, positive post from someone, whether I know them or not, I smile and think...there's a lightworker.

They have chosen to see life in a positive way.

I will feel the joy in their post, which will make me smile, which brightens the light within me. And so it goes, and so it goes.

Every time we see something wonderful or funny (not satire. Not about other people's misfortune, not your sarcasm), but truly funny, we FEEL the joy.

A smile is a muscle/brain reaction to happy.

Happy is a direct response to feeling positive.

Positivity is a choice.

A choice is the decision you make about how to proceed.

So why would anyone choose to proceed through a day, or a job, or a dilemma, with anything BUT the perception of a positive outcome?

Do you see how simple it is to grow light?

Do you understand now how important it is not to share negativity?

We want to be happy. All of us. It's a universal desire.

When I see people gathered, sharing love, laughter, and joy, even if I don't know them, the urge to join into that group is strong within me, and that's because true happiness is a physical emotion.

You draw to you, that which you give out.

You want to bitch and moan and curse the world? That is your choice. But understand that you will never find your way out of disappointment and darkness when you are sitting within turmoil and despair.

So know that your sweet posts and positive Memes, and your ability to laugh at yourself, and your willingness to share knowledge and help in a desire to relieve problems or other people's suffering, is turning on the light within you by the megawatts.

Thank you for your willingness to stand above the fray of discord.

Thank you for spreading light along MY path as I share MY light with you.

God sees your light.

And the Angels surround you in delight.

And you have just grown your soul in myriad ways.

Which is what you came here to do.

§&.

For every crime that goes unpunished, rest easy.

God's got this.

For every pain that goes unhealed, rest easy.

God's on it.

For every heartache that goes unheeded, rest easy.

God's there for you.

Lose the guilty conscience about not fighting every battle, marching in every march, picketing, not participating in every letter-writing campaign to right the wrongs in this world.

Look at your insular world and be at peace within it.

Focus on loving you and yours. Being present in their lives. Exerting effort within your own circle to bring peace and calm.

It all starts from home.

Everyday...today, tomorrow, and beyond, the password is LOVE.

Don't forget it.

You never know when you might need to use it.

§&.

Once in a while, I feel like I might be missing something important in the 27 years I've been published.

So many of my writer friends travel to distant lands, soaking up everything they see for research.

So many others I know pack up their laptops daily and go somewhere else to write. Somewhere fun. Somewhere public, where they drink lattes and eat yummy muffins still warm from the ovens.

Others travel in groups of three or more with their writer friends and have writing retreats. They do spa days and find wonderful places to sample local cuisine, all in the name of research.

Some of my writer friends go on cruises...others rent luxury hotel suites and write until they've finished what they went there to do.

I even know some writers who have hired guides and backpacked into rough terrains, all for their work in progress.

I write in my living room on my laptop, kicked back in my recliner, and when I need research, I Google it. In old fashioned journalism style, I find at least three answers to my question from different sites, to verify what I need to know.

When I'm tired of writing in my recliner with the laptop, I go into the office and write on my PC, sitting in the old office chair I've had for almost 20 years.

I don't have writing partners. In fact, I rarely talk to anyone during the day unless I leave the house. I see no one unless I leave my house.. There are no yummies in my house unless I cheat on my diet and make them.

Truth? I hate to travel.

I like being home. Where it's quiet. And no one interrupts my train of thought.

I would be miserable on a cruise because I'm afraid of dark water.

I have no sense of adventure anymore.

But I still have the gift God gave me.

I can still tell stories, and when I think about maybe traveling to some country I always wanted to see...I discard the thought and just write about it, instead.

I tell you all this...not because I'm complaining in any way, but as a way for you to see how different we all are as people, and yet how alike. Writers are dreamers. Storytellers. They come in all ages, with a shared and single focus...to be able to share the stories they write with people who love to read, and how they accomplish our goals is solely on them.

And I tell you, to illustrate to any men or women who are sitting in their homes tonight, imagining what it would be like to chase their dreams, and then talking themselves out of it because they think they have to be a certain way, look a certain way, live a certain way to make it happen.

But it's not about any of that. What you want comes from within you. From an overwhelming desire to be something other than who/what you are. With the gut instinct to realize that the only person stopping you is you. And with a faith in yourself that far outweighs the critics who will cross your path time and time again, trying to knock you off the ride you're on.

So let them try.

And if you fall, get up and keep moving.

They can't make you quit when it's your path, and your dream, and you're the one behind the wheel.

§♣

Nothing you do is wasted.

Not even what people call, wasting time.

Everything is either a learning experience, or the downtime you need to process it.

Stop pressuring yourself to be this great over-achiever.

No matter how much money you accumulate, or how many accolades and titles you can claim to your name, at the end of it all, what you did in the name of Love is all that is going to matter.

§♣

Ate Sunday dinner with Kathy and family again after LOVE Church. This time she made spinach/cheese quiche and a tossed salad...then had cookies made with three kinds of chocolate chips.

I got family hugs, a wonderful dinner, puppy kisses, and happy in my heart coming home.

It felt like when I was a little girl and we'd go to Grand and Grampy's after church and have Sunday dinner.

It is never about what you have to eat. It's being with people you love, and enjoy spending time with. It's grounding and resets my outlook on what really matters.

And for the person preparing the meal, it's renewing their spirit to cook and feed their tribe, whether it's blood kin or not.

When you sit around a table at home, the spirits of your loved ones are there, seeing the adults their loved ones have become, and feeling joy that their love and sacrifices were not in vain, and that we got what they were trying to teach us.

I know this isn't everybody's story, but it's mine, and I share it with you, because you're all part of my tribe, and I have love in my heart for you as well.

This coming week is going to be busy for me, but then most weeks are. Scout's birthday is this coming Friday. He'll be 17 years old. I can't believe it's been that long, but I'm very proud of the young man he is becoming. A gentle spirit and a good heart will carry him far in this world, because the world is changing/shifting into a higher dimension of energy where love and kindness is the norm, and he's SO already there.

Keep the faith that what you're doing at this moment is what you are meant to be doing.

If you're not in a place of peace, then you are in a place of learning. Every bit of our life on earth is either/or.

The weather cycles.

The seasons cycle.

The tide cycles daily as it ebbs and flows.

Our life from birth to going home is one cycle after another.

There's no such thing as always having bad luck.

If you are in the habit of saying stuff like..."if I didn't have bad luck, I'd have no luck at all, then kick the habit, because every time you say that, the Universe hears it as a request and gives you more of the same.

That's why your cycle is a continuation of tears or pain.

Be grateful each day for what you have, however sparse, however small, and the Universe will see your gratitude, and hear your dreams for more, or for a better life, and the opportunities to make that happen will show up in your path.

But...even though the opportunities arise to better your life will appear, it is ultimately up to you to choose them...It's all about free will.

God does not cause anything, or punish anyone.

But He's always there for love and support.

It's our freewill, and the life lessons we came to learn that set us on our paths.

୬

We came here with a soul contract to accomplish certain things.

God gave us free will and His LOVE...and asked only one thing of us. "Love one another, as I have loved you."

Seems simple enough

So as we muddle through life, we throw the word Love around like we're sowing wheat in earth unprepared for planting.

I love chocolate.

I love country music.

I love that perfume.

I just love the way she does my hair.

I love my job.

I love my family.

I love fried chicken.

I love pecan pie.

I love my pastor's sermons.

I love the way he sings.

I love my kids coach.

I love this car.

I love this dress so much.

I love this diamond ring.

I love to dance.

I love the way my honey hugs me.

I love my Granny's cooking.

I love the way my mother does my hair.

I love to travel.

I love to read.

I love the beach...

etc,

etc,

etc.

But we did not, nor have we ever, "loved one another as God loves us."

One thing.

He asked only one thing of us, and we didn't do it, because we broke another rule. We judge each other, and because we aren't all alike, we shun.

"Judge not, lest ye also be judged."

And yet...we do it anyway because...free will and fear.

Look at what's happening. Look at where we are. We became less than what was expected, and we want, without gratitude for what we already have.

Stop wanting, and start doing.

In the name of God, for God, just LOVE EACH OTHER for the humanity that we share.

🙢

This is not aimed at any one person.

I was doing research for a book and came across some stories of women in prison who got there, not because of something they did, but because they were living with someone who committed the crimes. It made them accomplices, even though they didn't know he was stashing stolen money in her apartment. And another was dealing drugs out of their home while she was at work, and so it went, and I couldn't get it out of my head. What on earth would possess a sane woman to hook up with a known criminal? Do they belittle the crimes in their minds just so they can okay his presence in their lives? Or are they just that pitiful...that they'll take anyone regardless?

These are women with no faith in themselves.

These are women who want someone to love them;

These are women who think a man will fix what's wrong in their lives.

These are women who believe they don't deserve anything but leftovers.

And it makes me--Sick. Sad. Mad.

I don't care what life has done to you in the past, I can tell you if you're in this situation right now...whatever has happened to you before, is nothing compared to what you have just done to yourself.

When you go looking for a mate for life, you do not shop in the ex-con aisle.

When you are looking for someone to date, if you have to write letters to them in prison, ask yourself why you're willing to settle for so much less.

When you think so little of yourself that you'll take the first guy who comes along and feeds you lies you so desperately want to believe, ask yourself if these are the guys you want your daughters to date.

Yes, all people deserve second chances, but when they are repeat offenders, you're out of your mind. You can't save him from himself and he doesn't need to change as long as he can con women like you who are desperate for love.

The people who help men like that are parole officers. You're not his parole officer. Why did you decide to go all Mother Teresa and save him, when you can't take care of yourself without help? What do you honestly think you're going to do to rehab a perp with a rap sheet longer than your arm?

And why, in the name of all that's holy, did you decide it was your duty to be the one who would certainly save him?

You are a means to an end to him. If he doesn't have a job. If he doesn't own a car. If he has kids he isn't allowed to see, then why in the name of God, are you willing to have your kids around him?

When you wind up as an accomplice in his next crime, there won't be anyone stepping up to help you, because you were warned.

Grown woman.

Free will.

Free choice.

No get out of jail free card for you.

You don't have to believe me.

Ask those women who are spending the most precious years of their lives behind bars.

❦

In peace I walk.

In love I walk.

Thinking of you.

Praying for you.

Feeling your troubles.

Seeing your pain.

Hearing the heartache in your voice when you whisper a name.

You don't have to whisper, even if they're gone.

They hear you, they see you, you are never alone.

This is the way God sees us.

Laughing joyously.

Enraged with anger.

Broken by heartaches.

Beaten down by pain.

He knows you've forgotten that this was what you came here to do.

He hears you cry out for mercy, and for healing.

He hears you whisper His name.

He hasn't forgotten you.

He's is simply honoring the choices where your free will took you.

If you heal, it was what you were meant to do.

And if you don't, He's waiting with love to bring you home.

Understand this:

God is not orchestrating our lives.

We are.

Our angels surround us always while we're here.

Often they are the ones who step in and work the miracles that befall us, because it wasn't yet our time to go.

And sometimes it's our loved ones in spirit who are with us in our darkest hours.

We did not come here for smooth sailing. That's where we came from.

Here is school. Here is learning and sometimes repeating the lessons lifetime after lifetime until we get it right.

You are a bright and shining light.

Don't cover yourself up with the darkness of fear.

Remember: This is not forever.

And trying to stop the hands of time is futile.

Don't grieve the loss of your youth.

Rejoice in the wisdom of age.

Wrap the life you've lived around you like a familiar blanket, ignore the raveled edges, for they were valiantly earned.

Wear your scars like badges.

Appreciate the life you're living, no matter how long it will be.

Know the slowing steps you know take aren't to burden you, but to help you through the fall and winter of life.

Human is here.

Forever is there, and the door is always open.

෴

Today was a first for me.

I cried reading a magazine. I know. But crying isn't always about sadness. Sometimes something is so beautiful, or so touching that you have to cry or die from the way it felt as you read.

It wasn't some big, literary piece, and it wasn't some story about how someone survived a dramatic event.

It was a simple picture, and the story that went with it. Just the back view of a mother and her teenage daughter walking, with the mother's hand on her daughter's back, as if she'd just reached out in a subconscious way, wanting to hold onto her, but knowing the daughter's path was leading away from home.

It was in the fall issue of The Pioneer Woman magazine, and the picture was of Ree Drummond and her daughter, Paige, who just went away too college. Ree has four children, two girls, who are her two eldest, and two boys, who are still living at home.

I felt the poignancy so deeply as she talked about now living in a house full of men and boys, and how she was missing her daughter.

It's a valid thing...to identify with your own sex. Even when you love all your children so deeply, and would die to protect any of them, it's the girls who "get" Mama, and it's Mama who "gets" the girls.

So I cried.

And now writing this, I am crying again because the feeling of mutual understanding is so deep and ingrained in me.

These are the moments in my day that always draw me back to what matters in life, and that's loving myself, and loving my children and their children, and being proud of their choices in life, and knowing all of the wear and tear on a mother's heart that goes with raising them was worth it.

I have never--not once--doubted the people they became. Their life choices as adults, have always been at the highest good, and have never made me ashamed, or given me cause to doubt them. That's what a mother aims for--knowing that the children she raised respect themselves enough not to ever put themselves or their children in harm's way.

So this is a good day. And to make it even better, I've already had a Mama kiss and hug from my daughter. My son is dropping by shortly to eat Hideaway Pizza. I'll get a Mama kiss and hug from him, too, and I think my baby girl, Crissy, will drop by or call later today, and I'll get an Auntie kiss from her, too.

You can't give me a day better than this.

&

I am going to get my hair done this morning.

It will be a good thing to get away for a bit from the ugly and snide little Memes going around right now, all referencing women who have been assaulted.

I'm still in shock, and wondering why so many women are the ones sharing them.

I can't imagine being callous enough to make fun of someone else's tragedy.

I don't understand the people who do.

I expected a lot of protest and whining to come from some men, but as jaded as I am about this world right now, it caught me off guard to see the same memes being passed around and laughed at by women, too.

This isn't me calling anyone out.

This is me being disheartened and sad that it is happening.

All I know is...if it ever happened to them, they wouldn't be laughing. If it happened to their daughters or to their mothers, they wouldn't be laughing.

What they don't realize is all of their finger pointing and laughing only says to me how scared they are, and makes me wonder how many of them have been victims and have never told.

If this is the case, you need to know that your loud voice in this area only brings all the focus up to you, and leaves people wondering if you protest too loudly, in order to shed the light on everyone else.

If this is the case, you should feel no shame. You would be a victim, not the perpetrator...which is the exact behavior you exhibit by making fun of some in the sisterhood of women.

I'm not bringing this up for discussion.

I am simply pointing this out to you, so that you understand how your behavior gives other women this impression.

It is always your choice to do as you wish.

And while the wise thing would be to stay silent if you are trying to mask your truth with ugly behavior toward other woman, and I do understand how trauma makes everyone react in different ways.

But just for today, why don't you try deleting the hateful meme instead of commenting on it, or sharing it and laughing even louder.

Why don't you just try it?

See how freeing that makes you feel not to be involved in causing others pain.

Sending blessings to all...and today...sending special blessings of love and peace in your hearts to my soul sisters who are in pain.

≷⬤

When the chaos of life seems overwhelming:
Instead of sinking, I rise.
I do one thing positive for me.
I do one thing positive for someone I love.
I do one thing positive for a stranger.

There is no reason whatsoever to let yourself be swamped by sadness or bitterness from your past, when the future is always a change waiting to happen.

If it pleases you to stay in a place of anger, then it is done.

If it pleases you to demand all others think your way, then it is done.

If it pleases you to discriminate and belittle, then it is done.

What you choose, and how you behave are the signals to the Universe as to what you will get.

And it is done.

Whether you like it or not, everyone has the right to their own opinion. God gave them that. He called it free will.

So every time you rage and discriminate against another person just because their choice was not yours, you are saying that God was wrong and you are right. Really? Is that the only thing you can think to do.

Stop talking.
Walk away.
Remove yourself from the argument.
You're meddling in God's business.
It's not your war to fight.

≷⬤

I am helping Crissy move this morning.
No, I'm not lifting anything. We hired a mover, but I'll be on my feet way more than is comfortable...so by the time I get home this afternoon, I seriously doubt if you'll hear from me.

The birthday dinner we had for Scout last night was a huge success. He is now officially 17.

We tried out the new restaurant/brewery on Main Street in Norman, called The Winston. Scout picked it out. Probably because it's the same name as his Winston puppy.

No.. I take that back. He's something of a gourmet and I think he probably read the menu, because he had chicken-fried quail, (tiny little drumsticks) and Jalapeno cheese grits with a bomb of a marinara dipping sauce.

I had an amazing cup of vegetable quinoa stew and a small order of garlic cheese flatbread to go with it, Ash order a steak and fries, and Kathy, always the venturous one like Scout, ordered a pulled meat sandwich called the Chupacabra. LOLOL It was somewhat spicy, she said, and fries with that.

I will definitely go there again for that vegetable stew. It was a mouthful of flavor in every bite...even if I did sort out most of the chopped avocado that was in it and leave it on the plate beneath. I don't much care for it, and even though I tried it two or three times in a bite with the rest of the veggies, it still had a gel-like grease taste to me and nothing else, because it doesn't absorb flavors.

Find the positive in your day, and when it happens, smile.

It's a reminder to you that there are plenty of things to smile about every day, but not everybody takes the time to appreciate them.

Over and out.

See you on the other side....

❧

I had to read myself the riot act this morning.

I had to finally cry, just to get rid of what I've been feeling.

I've had to come to terms with decisions others made that will ultimately affect me as well, without taking it into my heart.

Obviously, their choices are theirs to make, but they made them knowing I would have no part of it.

So their choice has been made.

And such is life.

Holidays will be different.

I have yet to figure out what that even means.

I just know that it's sad.

They have what they want, but at a price.

That's how life goes.

Sometimes it works.

And sometimes love isn't enough.

Sometimes you're so broken you can't see danger for the blood already in your eyes.

But, that's not my path to walk, or to interfere.

Time is immeasurable.

There is either never enough, or you can't wait for something to be over.

It's endless to children and too brief for parents.

It goes so slow when you're young, and the older you get, the faster it moves, taking you with it at breakneck speed, changing your world every minute, every hour, every day.

Some days you make a plan, and then time runs out to see it through, or it turned out to be a bad idea and then you're bemoaning all the time you think you wasted.

But time is never wasted.

Whatever you're doing, your time is being spent in learning.

Just remember what works and what doesn't, and don't repeat your mistakes.

❦

Lord, what a day.

Got up and baked the cookies I posted pictures of earlier, delivered tax papers for mother and me to my CPA. Then grabbed lunch for Kathy and me and ate with her at school. I came home tired and hurting. And I still needed to clean up the cookie baking mess. By the time I was finished, my foot was aching.

I stretched out in the recliner with my laptop playing my music to heal inflammation, and about mid-way through the hour long piece, I fell asleep and woke up to gongs and bells, and a whole other kind of music. I'd slept through my music and it automatically played the next one. LOL Talk about waking up confused.

But I felt better. My foot had quit hurting, and I made myself an early supper. Now I'm waiting for The Voice to come on at 7:00.

I might even get a little writing done tonight.

I feel like I'm in a holding pattern, so my ability to focus is challenged, at best.

But, stuff does happen, whether I'm ready for it or not, and life does go on.

The one positive in my life is my home and the quiet. I need that.

If I have one more disaster this month I might turn in my resignation. If I can find someone to take it. That's the downside of being your own boss. LOL

The biggest, most exciting news in the state is being able to sell beer and 'fine wine' in grocery stores. I guess it's all about priorities.

I have no further comment.

Tomorrow is my day to get a massage. I go twice a month to Energy Massage and let Delinda work her magic on all the kinks in my shoulders and back, and rub the aches right out of my body. It is better than a shot in the arm and a prescription from a doctor, any day.

This week, it has been brought home to all of us how quickly life can change.

Don't waste time being angry.

Don't miss your chance to hug your loved ones.

I made peace with myself.

We don't come with expiration dates, so we live as if we're immortal.

Maybe we wouldn't be so quick to abandon one thing for another because the new thing looked shiny, if we could only see how rich we already are in what matters.

It's always about choice and free will, but I'll add one more facet to that.

Finish what you start.

§•

Having lunch today with two writers, Karen Crane, who used to write as Karen Toller Whittenburg, from the Tulsa area, and Paula

Hamilton, who lives in Texas. It's always good times when writers get together.

I intend to finish a chapter today in my WIP. (work in progress)

When Bobby and I were out on the ranch, I sat in the living room on a big sectional sofa to write, and all I had to do was look up and to my left through the wide picture window to see the ranch. There were horses in the land across the road, and there were horses in the pastures behind the house, and to the east of the house. Two barns sat on the east and I was surrounded by acres and acres of woodland and pasture. Wild turkeys were common, as were deer. They were often scattered among the horse herd, so that it wasn't easy to see whether it was deer or horses when the day was coming to an end.

Often I would be so deep into the story I was writing that I wouldn't know Bobby had come in the back door until he leaned over the back of the sofa and hugged me, or kissed me on the back of my neck. Sometimes now when I'm writing, I can almost feel his cold nose and warm lips on the back of my neck, and hear the deep rumble of his laughter near my ear.

Now I write facing a wall and a TV, but that's okay, because there's nothing of interest for me to see out my windows here. Just concrete and houses.

My life changed, but my path did not.

I still believe Love is the way.

Loving each other.

Honoring the humanity in each of us.

And staying on a path of purpose.

❦

An advertising slogan in my Spam email gave me a laugh this morning.

"Has Mahnolo Blahnik ever let you down?" was the slogan, of course advertising the 3 and 4 inch heels on the designer shoes.

But me, being me, my first thought was, "No, because I was never married to him." I laughed at myself, and then as I thought about that,

I realized how jaded that sounded and forgave myself. Life experience gives us our dialog and thoughts.

Shoes were never a thing for me, so I'm afraid I'll be the one letting Mahnolo down. Sorry, Dude. It's not you. It's me.

It's raining here this morning...a long line of thunderstorms is moving through the state. The storm front has already moved past me, but not before we got a tornado warning. The storm is spawning little tornadoes that drop down at intermittent points along the line. It appears the storm is increasing in intensity as it moves further East. It's moving through the area in the northern part of the state where my son lives, and reaches all the way down through the middle and southern part of the state, moving east. It's moving through the Prague area, where I used to live, toward Paden in Okfuskee country, where I grew up. Sending prayers for everyone to be safe. <3

Be at peace within yourselves today.

There is change in the air, even if you can't see it, many of us already feel it.

Don't focus on what's already been said and done.

Know that your voices were heard.

Know that the Lightworkers diligence to growing light with love was, and is still, the strong but silent wind that lifted peace far above the drums of war.

The energy in our dimension has changed, and the power darkness held over us in the past is fading away.

Believe in you and your power to accomplish anything you wish.

Believe that peace and love accomplish far more in the long run than angry words spoken in a rush.

We are now living in a higher level of energy.

The past has no place here.

That belonged to before.

This is now.

This is me loving you.

*

Today would have been Daddy's 99th birthday.

He was the first man I loved, and I'm thinking of you with love, Daddy...remembering all the funny stuff, and all the loving stuff, and the scent of your Old Spice and the pipe tobacco.

The sound of your laugh, and how tall you stood within this world.

My first view of the world was from my Daddy's shoulders.

It was a beautiful sight to behold.

Today is also the CORRECT day to have lunch with Karen and Paula. They've already sent me a text that they're on their way, but they're coming from Tulsa, so it will be a bit before they arrive. We're going to have such a good time catching up. Writers never run out of stuff to say. LOL

Yesterday, someone suggested something very intriguing to me. So much so, that I will be implementing this into my daily life.

Every day, I am going to envision how I WANT my life to be within this world. And then I am going to envision it as already being a fact.

Everything from my health, to my work life, to my family's well-being, to comfort, to happiness, to fulfillment, to joy.

I am going to create my new space and in doing so, will be helping build a new world, a better world.

If each of us thought of life as having purpose and helping others, what's happening in the world would not exist.

And since Earth and everything on it is pure energy (including us), if I raise my energy, I help raise it for others. And if they raise theirs, then even more feel better, which gives them the push they need to raise their own. To live outside the confines of debt and taxes. To live where health care is the same for everyone, and no one goes homeless or hungry.

You think it can't happen?

If you think that way, I guarantee it won't happen for you.

What better way to use your thoughts, than in positive purpose.

I won't waste my thoughts on revenge.

Or on the past.

Or what went wrong in my life.

Or what link in a family/friendship/loving chain was broken.

Because that's before.

This is now.

I want now to be better than before, and the only way I make that happen for me, is to create my own reality.

If you continue to look back, and choose discord instead of discourse, nothing will change.

ᢓᢀ

This morning is a chilly, rainy morning...and I can't help thinking what the latest victims of Hurricane Michael are enduring right now. My love, prayers for healing, and prayers for recovery are with them. There has been so much hardship this year involving weather related events, and accidents. So many, too many, for the heartaches of families enduring it all.

October is almost halfway gone and it feels like it was just the first of the month yesterday. I always heard that the older you get, the faster life goes, and I know now that's so true.

But it's nothing to regret. It's all about rejoicing that I have survived it, and that I'm still on my path.

I'm drinking my morning Plexus protein shake, as usual. Already drank my Slim. Yes, I still use those products. I will until I drop because they healed parts of me that had been out of rhythm for most of my life. I used to worry about losing weight, losing weight--always trying one diet or another and looking for the cheap fix.

What I know now is that it's not about the weight loss...it's about getting healthy. The weight loss takes care of its self when that happens. And no, it wasn't easy, but boy, was it worth it.

It's a good thing I finally found someone to fix my sewing machine because Crissy brought over a pair of jeans and a pair of tights for me to fix last night. When I die, Kathy gets that sewing machine. She's the only other member of my family who learned to sew and liked it. All those years of 4-H club. Someone has to be able to still sew up the rips in the family britches when I'm gone. LOL

I will be baking something I don't need today, but it will freeze. That's what my mother was always doing. She baked several days a week. She was the cookie queen, always taking cookies to the post office for the workers, and to first one friend or another around town. She was such a busy, loving little thing. And she's still a busy loving little thing, even if she doesn't remember, because even at her care center, she's never still. <3

The message for this morning was brief, but to the point. No mistaking the urgency either, when I heard it. So here it is:

It is in your best interests to stay positive in the days to come.

It matters that you care about others.

Love one another.

Do no harm.

⚘

Women:

Why do you compare yourself to another?

Why can you not seek the things within you that you admire?

Why do you belittle others by demeaning their own choice of style?

Are you so insecure within yourself that you can't be satisfied until you have pulled another sister woman down to your level of dissatisfaction?

You hold up one woman's clothing style against another woman's clothing style, and then proceed to tear them apart, belittling, demeaning, laughing at what they chose, picking apart their choice of hair style, their makeup, whether they look fat or are too skinny.

You turn yourself into Cinderella's step-sisters, highlighting your jealousy and shaming yourself in the process.

Those women don't know you're doing it, so they're not hurt in the process.

But you've shown your true self to everyone else who does know you, and it is not a pretty picture.

It is time in this world to stop the bullshit.

Stop the ridicule.

Stop the shaming.

Stop the judging.

If you can't be happy with who you are and the path you are on,

Making fun of others won't change what's wrong with your world.
Stand in front of a mirror in what YOU'RE wearing.
Then look at yourself.
Pick yourself apart, discard what displeases you, and make the changes YOU need to be happy.
Don't drag your sister friend down.
Don't throw shade.
Don't envy.
Be the light.
Said with love,
Sent with love.

❧

There are people who live their lives for others. They've lost their way and their sense of self.

I know that life. I lived it.

It is often an empty life, celebrating others accomplishments, living for the random compliments that come your way.

It's not a bad thing, but it is a very sad thing, because we did not come here to be invisible.

If this is you right now, read my words.

I SEE YOU, MY SISTER.

I know your heart.

I dreamed your dreams and cried those same tears.

And I didn't know how to change, either.

But I wanted to, and one day when someone volunteered me for a task without even asking me, I spoke up and said, NO.

I said I was busy that day.

It was the most daring, freeing thing I'd ever done. That one small thing. But it changed my life.

I know it was spirit saying to me, "It is time to step out of the shadows. You have much work yet to do."

And so I stepped, found my path, and for the first time in my life I was moving forward.

It shocked some. Angered others. And I was judged and highly disapproved of.

Didn't care. Didn't look back. You don't have to look back when you are no longer in shadows, because there is nothing behind you but the light you are leaving as you pass along the way.

We're all on our journeys.

If I pass you on your path,

I WILL SEE YOU.

I will know you as a kindred spirit.

A good woman.

A woman who is on her path, leaving light behind her as she goes to shine the light for others.

Just as I do, so can you.

&

I had an early hair appointment. Just a cut and style, but then what seemed like a dozen little to-do things, then hurried home, got a package ready to mail and went back out in the rain to send it off. At 2:30, I finally made myself lunch and sat down to eat. I'm tired and haven't hit a lick of writing today, so that will mean a late night.

It's chilly and drizzling again today, so I broke out the raincoat to do all my running around, and bought two new umbrellas at the grocery store because I had given all of mine away. It's just something I do when it's raining and I see people on the streets who are obviously without cars, and either sitting on a bench waiting for a bus, (yes, we only have a few bus stops in the city that are covered. All the rest are just benches.) or walking in it without anything to protect them. I had even given my own umbrella away, so now I'm stocked back up again.

Just a few minutes ago I was listening to my healing music on YouTube, when my ears suddenly popped and drowned out all sound, then seconds later, YouTube went down and wouldn't come back up. So I just rolled my eyes and shifted to posting here instead. This energy shift has played heck with my technology. I have an older television in my living room and it goes off all the time, and then resets it's self. I'm going to have to break down and get a new TV one of these days so it will work with the new levels. My newer, smaller TV in my bedroom doesn't do this, which tells me it's the age of the television that's probably causing it.

Every day I hold onto two things.

My belief in the Universe and the Great I Am,

And the path I am on.

It is important to know your own truth.

It is more important to live it, regardless of what others think.

I didn't come here just to make friends.

But I did come with so much LOVE to share.

I am full to overflowing with Love for all of you who have become so dear to me.

I cry when you cry.

I grieve your losses.

I celebrate your successes.

I understand your frustrations.

And I know how hard it is to start over...again and again.

But the gratitude I hold for the hard times, is that I had the strength and courage to do it.

Always, my goal is to do no harm.

To say nothing purposefully hurtful, but at the same time, I will speak the hard truths, and this is one.

You will never move forward, if you continue to choose second best. We all deserve to be honored. But if you are not living an honorable life, you are the one holding yourself back.

Said with love.

Sent with love.

&.

Accepting what we view as our physical flaws is the first step to happiness.

Once you realize we can't all be alike, and that we're genetically linked to every ancestor we ever had, short or tall, wide or thin, elegant or awkward, then you begin to understand the assortment of who we are. Like bits and pieces of old clothing that became quilt squares, and then a new, beautiful quilt, so then are we.

I am grateful to be connected to all who came before me, and I know their hopes and dreams for the future generations had nothing to do with pretty hair and lithe bodies, and neither should ours.

Striving to be healthy is what we all hope for.

Striving only for physical beauty is a wasted life.

Said with love.

Sent with love.

❧

When I was little, I used to go with my Grampy to his workshop when he had to fire up the forge to fix a piece of machinery that broke. I'd work the bellows when he told me to..and Lord, yes, it was hot in there, and all my long curly hair was in my face and stuck to my fore-head with sweat, but I couldn't have been happier.

That's where he also fixed the family shoes. If someone had a sole come loose, or needed a new one put on, he took the shoe...and me...because nosy might need to see how all that worked and he didn't care...and sat down at his work bench and slid the shoe over a little pedestal he'd made for just that purpose, so that the sole was facing up. I'd watch him clean, then trim, then get his little hammer and the tiniest little nails, and start putting the sole back on. Sometimes the shoes were so thin that a tiny point would come through into the shoe, but he knew how to fix that too.

Depending on how much had come through, he either took tiny needle nose pliers and bent it over, then hammered it flat, or took some tiny shears and just cut off the point.

I'd say, "Grampy, are we done now?"

And he would say, "Almost, sugar. We're going to put a new insole into the shoe, too. He'd already traced the shoe sole onto brown felt...Originally one of his felt hats and now the source of insole fabric. Once it was cut out, he'd work and work trimming it down until it was a perfect fit inside the shoe. At that point, he'd glue it down, covering up and padding the place where the nail had come through. Then we were done. He carried it back into the house to dry, and I remember Grand exclaiming over what a good job he'd done, and praising him for saving them the money it would have cost to have a cobbler do it in town.

I tell you this story, because last year the heel on the sole of a good pair of my shoes came loose. I tried to get it fixed, but it didn't hold, so I put them up. I wear the left side of every shoe I own down, before the rest. Corrective insoles stopped that, but now I can't wear the shoes those insoles once fit, because of my constantly sore feet. One foot continues to have mild RA flares and a little bit of swelling in the ankle, but even when it's not swollen, it's very tender to the touch.

And yesterday, my right foot, which has been minding its own business for two years without issue, decided to have a gout flare. I couldn't believe it. There's no explanation for it other than my body said, "Oh screw it, she needs something else to think about, and it throbbed all night and is tender today, as well.

So I'm getting ready to go to Urgent Care (my regular doctor has two hours of office on Friday and then he's gone). It's pouring rain. I can't wear the half-assed shoes I've been wearing out and about because they're fabric, not leather.

This morning, I looked at that downpour, and my two sore feet, and thought of those good shoes with the flapping rubber heel and said... "I can fix this because I watched my Grampy do it."

I got out my picture hanging equipment, a small hammer from my tool box, and chose the tiniest little nails in the box. They're about an inch long. No more, and I knew if this worked, they wouldn't go through into the inside of the shoe.

So, with my Grampy looking over my shoulder...and don't scoff...I felt every loving moment of his presence and knew he was pleased that I'd remembered...I fixed my shoe. No it's not pretty, but it worked, my foot didn't hurt, and it held up like a Boss out in that rain.

Yes, I could have gotten new shoes, but who would break them in? I can't. And I don't believe in throwing something good and wearable away just because something broke.

I know how to fix shit.

Posting a picture.

If I could still dance, I'd wear the shine right off those little nails tonight.

ᥫ

Today has been a gift of blessings. The steroid shot I got yesterday allowed me enough pain relief to enjoy this day. I wanted to go to Willams-Sonoma in Penn Square Mall, and Kathy took me today. We both LOVE going in that store. All the baking things and kitchen stuff. We each came home with a new baking pan from Nordic Ware and I did a little Christmas shopping there, too. Had to stop at the kiosk in the mall and get a 6 pack of Macarons...I'm glad that place is too far away for me to make that a habit. LOL

We ate lunch at Texas de Brazil at the mall before we came home. Their salad bar is huge, and we both skipped the meat service, which is their featured draw. I took a picture of the massive floral decoration above one of two parts of the salad bar. It's just a glorious mass of blooms.

I'm including a picture of Kathy and I. We were color coordinated by accident. We do that often. But I can tell you right now I'm taking the scissors to that pink shirt of mine and making it about a three inch hem shorter. If I had the guts to wear tights, that thing could pass for a dress. But I digress.

It's good to step back now and then and see what grows in this world, and admire the skill of people who can create such displays.

This morning I stopped to get gas before I went to Kathy's, and as I was looking up, I gasped. The sky was full of clouds that ALL looked like feathers.... And there's one more picture I took at my house a few days of that is also of clouds...and something else. I'm sure you'll see it. I call it my Hand of God picture.

Of course we had to stop in the Lego store in the mall when we were leaving. Conveniently, it's the store next to Williams-Sonoma. LOL I say had to, because EVERY TIME Scout goes to the mall, he brings me back a 6 pack of macarons. So this time, I picked out a Lego set and sent it home with Kathy. Reciprocating a kindness isn't gifting.

It's a sign of appreciation for the thoughtfulness of someone so young, who already displays a loving and generous heart.

In this world, there can never be too much kindness given, or love displayed. Everywhere you go in life, you are leaving an imprint of you in someone's eyes or someone's heart and you don't even know it. But your soul knows, and God knows, and as you are growing your light and growing your soul, you are also lifting someone else up enough to help them grow, too.

Said with love,

Sent with love.

Life isn't about parties, fun, and pretty clothes.

It isn't about fancy cars and chasing the best looking partners.

Ask yourself why you feel the need to seek fulfillment in festivities, when the things that feed your soul come from the still, quiet places in your heart.

Off to LOVE church in a bit and then having lunch at Kathy's house with Ash, and Scout...and the three doggies, too.

It is a day for thanksgiving...to have friends in God and family, too.

Even if you are in a daily struggle with life, use today as a springboard to acceptance with where you are.

Only after you learn to be at peace with where your choices have taken you, can you see the opening in the path where you want next want to go.

Life is a journey, not a place to be.

Home is what you carry in your heart, and wherever you are, is where you belong.

Today is Tuesday with Kathy.

Egg salad sandwiches and Fritos by request.

She is her mama's daughter. LOL

I now own a potted plant too big for my house. I put it outside this spring when it became warm enough.

Ash just brought it back in for the winter.

It no longer fits the spot it was in, and there aren't others that work.

argh...

I'm not even a plant in the house person, because I always forget to water them. The only thing I've had for any length of time is the Peace Lily someone gave me when Bobby died. That was 2005. I've re-potted it a couple of times, and I forget to water it on a regular basis. I should rename it a Resurrection plant (yes I know there really is a plant with this name, but this isn't it.) because when I finally do remember to water it, it resurrects itself and blooms like crazy. I just take it's continued persistence in my life as an analogy of Bobby's presence with me. Only an angel could keep a plant alive that's never fed or watered.

I had a dream last night that I was searching for a new house to live in. It was me and my kids. They were in their teens still, no families of their own. We saw a house that was huge...three stories...so many rooms, and despite the logistics of it, that's the one we chose.

So we moved in, and as we were putting things up, a large group of people walked by the house. They stopped, and were just standing in the road, looking at it. In the dream, my kids brought them inside and asked if they could stay because they didn't have homes anymore.

The most wonderful part of the dream was that all of a sudden me choosing that house made sense. We agreed it was a most logical decision, and I was happy that the excess in my life was going to be put to use.

We were living together without issue, blending knowledge and food and shelter, and our family of three had suddenly exploded in a huge family.

The house was full of light and laughter. When people spoke, their voices held joy and hope. When children played, their bellies weren't distended from starvation, and they ran with all the joy only children and puppies exhibit.

And then I woke up.

I like my dream better than I like this world.

As I continue to create MY vision of a new earth, I think I will incorporate living in this way as normal.

What good is a fancy car and fine clothes on one person, if ten are afoot and in rags?

There's not one commandment in anyone's Bible that says living in selfishness is okay.

"Do unto others, as you would have done unto you."

Said with love.

Sent with love.

§♠

Every phone call I have with my son always leaves me feeling blessed for getting to be his mother.

He called me this morning...he does that often..checking in on my welfare and on his grandmother. Little Mama.

We talk about all kinds of things afterward...about life, about life lessons, about what's going on with my granddaughters, about their college life and work, and I hear so much love for them in his voice. We are so connected in the family roots we nurture.

Sometimes he'll chuckle about something he had to repair at home, and I hear, in his calm, methodical way, telling about the pitfalls that kept happening as he went about it, and I feel as if I'm listening to my Grampy, who always found a way to make something work, and did it without anger or blame.

My son is the anchor in his family. He is the go-to man for answers. Even if they're hard to hear, he doles them out in the same calm, kind voice in which he holds conversation.

He is the solid rock on which his family stands.

He and I started our lives together as just the two of us, but the family we gathered along the way has blessed the both of us.

When you know who your people are, then you understand the beginning of you.

Why you aren't taller. Why your smile is always tilted a little bit sideways. Why your hair grows in a cowlick above your right eye. Why there's a slight cleft in your chin. Why you laugh or chew your food a certain way. Not everything is learned behavior. Some of it is inherent.

Instead of regretting anything you view as shortcomings...celebrate, instead, the blood you share, the bonds of family, even the roots that hold you fast against some of life's greatest storms.

Said with love.

Sent with love.

§

Yesterday was a whirlwind day of busy stuff.

Today is my day. A day of withdrawing into the quiet place I call home. Half of the morning is gone and I have yet to hear a voice other than my own...and I only spoke aloud during my daily affirmations.

Sometimes when a person isn't feeling well, or having a bad day at work simply from something that happened at home, the excess noise of voices and conversations around them at work only add to their already troubled emotions. It's not what they're hearing...it's just the noise.

We all need quiet to regroup.

To find our own center...it's like resetting a clock that's on the wrong time.

When I was a child, going to church on Sunday and sitting in the pew with my Grand on one side of me, and my Mother on the other was how my world reset itself. Despite whatever had happened during the past week, that morning of leaning my head against Grand's shoulder, or feeling Mother reach out and pat my arm or smile at me, was like a key unlocking the box where I'd put my troubles. Their presence and the love I felt from both of them gave me the freedom to release my childhood worries and woes. Nothing was wrong in my world when I was sitting between the two women who loved me most.

Even though there was a sermon in progress, Brother Farley's deep, sonorous voice drifted up into the high ceilings before the sounds came down to us. Hearing the word of God coming down from the ceiling was, in my childish mind, hearing God's own voice coming down from heaven.

I didn't always understand the messages. But I felt the peace and reassurance.

So today I am blessed with a day of solitude.

I will not dwell on troubles that are not my own.

I have given it all to the great I AM.

Today is for me.

Today I feed my soul.

Consider the possibility of finding even five minutes of your time today to let go of that which you cannot control.

Just close your eyes, take a deep breath, speak aloud your troubles, and then give them to God.

He is waiting.

Said with love.

Sent with love.

&a.

Spent a most uplifting two hours last night at a Leslie Draper gallery witnessing people getting messages and blessings from their loved ones who have passed.

If you've never been to anything like this.. You aren't alone.

But after you've experienced it once, you totally understand how near your loved ones always are. Even if you don't know it.

And even if you do.

Before I left the house, I said aloud, "I need help, and I need answers. Whoever is listening, you also know why. You know where I'm going tonight, so show up and help me. I guess I should have been more specific, because it seems I opened a floodgate.

My Daddy, my Bobby, my sister Diane, and my little Grand were all there. Leslie had no idea what I needed to know, but they did, and I got my answers. To all of it.

What I didn't expect were, what Leslie described as lines and lines of spirits I didn't know, who had come to thank me, because these posts I've been putting up, have helped their loved ones who are still here, accept, understand, and come to terms with, the grief they were suffering for losing them.

They all wanted to send messages back to their loved ones through me of how proud they were of their families for 'getting it', for understanding that they were gone because it was their time to go, or because they'd been in such a place of torment here, that they needed to go home to God.

But there was no time to intercede for such an endless line of Spirit.

So I want to say this now...and the ones who need to read this will understand it's meant for them.... If you have recently been able to come to terms with the loss of loved ones...even if they've been gone for a long time and you weren't able to get past YOUR loss to think of the blessing it was for THEM to leave...and that now you have released yourself from all grief or guilt surrounding their passing...THEY are so proud of you. They are blessed by your acceptance, because you have also released them of the last remnants of any guilt they might have carried for letting you down.

Everything in life and death always comes full circle.

{*

Happy birthday, Diane!

You and Daddy have been gone from us for thirty-three years.

You two were a hard act to follow.

I will do an act of random kindness to someone today in your memory.

Lord do I ever wish you were here. As you used to say, I'm up to my ass in alligators here. I sure could use your biting wit and big hugs.

We were total opposites in what we liked to do, and yet we had THE best time together. I think it was because of Daddy, right? We both got his big laugh and funny sense of humor.

Remember how we used to bust out laughing just by looking at each other? And how Mother sat between us in church because we invariably got the giggles at least once a Sunday over Mr. Bowman always falling asleep in church. We'd watch him nodding and nodding off and then his head would roll so far back his head would hit the end of the pew where he sat, and it would startle him awake.

And remember how we put birthday money in the little white plastic bank made to look like a church. Brother Farley would ask if anyone had a birthday and then they would raise their hand and get up and go down to the pulpit and put money in the bank that equaled their age. Remember the year I turned ten, and I was holding my ten pennies in my hand, then sneezed and dropped them, and all ten pennies loudly hit the floor and rolled all the way down the sloping floor to the pulpit with everyone laughing. We couldn't even look at each other without hysterics. Looking back, I imagine Mother wanted to brain us. (Her phrase for yanking a knot in our tails. LOL)

Anyway...I miss you and your silliness. And despite how much I hated shopping, I would so go look at stuff with you.

Remember the day we met up at the old Shepherd Mall in OKC?

We walked and walked and went through every freaking clothing store in the mall. You tried on one outfit after the other, with me tagging along for the thumbs up, or the thumbs down decisions. After three good hours of this, I finally said..."Lord have mercy, Diane. Make a decision here." And you turned and looked at me and said..."Oh..I can't buy anything. I'm broke. I just like to look."

So that's what I miss. Your ability to have fun no matter what was happening. You had that down to a science.

Love you.

Miss you.

Come get Mother.

She forgot the way home.

❧

I pray tonight as I lie down, that we will find a way to be at peace.

That we will find something we can love about each other as much as people love their pets.

I pray that people will choose to stay silent, rather than encroach on other people's FB pages and sound off, just because they can.

I pray that before I die, I will witness a measure of love and understanding among us.

I pray that the world I will be leaving will be better for my grand-daughters to raise their children, than the one I grew up in.

I do not fool myself in believing it will become a Shangri-La.

I would settle for a measure of consideration and the intelligence in knowing when to keep your mouth shut.

These aren't outrageous statements to make.

They could be solved right now if people didn't have the over-whelming need to always be right, even if it involved ignoring truth and believing lies to make it happen.

If just once they could accept they are allowed their truth, but then so is everyone else...allowed their truth.

My truth may never be your truth.

But that won't make me hate you.

That won't make me call you names.

That won't make me a bully to you.

It won't make me change the love God put in my heart when I was born.

I won't let ugly replace the beauty my eyes see in every face.

I won't let myself be swayed by the masses.

I am not afraid to stand alone in my truth.

I would be ashamed in the eyes of God if I did not stand fast to His word, just as firmly as I stand in His light.

Said with love.

Sent with love.

❧

My uncle Hubert passed last night.

He was Uncle Bee to me. (a nickname his mama gave him when he was just a little boy). He was the last one left of Daddy's five brothers, and now they're all together again, and Uncle Bee has been reunited with his twin brother. He sure did miss him. I can only imagine all the family who was waiting for him when he arrived.

My love and prayers are with Aunt Donna, with his son, Donnell, and Janette and their families. With his daughter, Christy, and Benny Jones and their families... Thank you, Shelby Smith, for letting us know last night. You always touch my heart with your devotion to your own sweet family.

And so it is. Another passing, but not a loss, because we didn't lose him. He left a bit of himself in all the memories of those of us who knew and loved him.

Nothing about his life was wasted.

He was a true and faithful man of God.

Today is also Tuesday with Kathy.

She lifts my heart.

She makes me smile.

Her eyes always light up as she's telling me a funny from one of the kids in her class.

Their logic is so honest...and even when they're trying to justify what they just pulled, or hoping to deny it with a shrug...she always turns the question around from a "Did you do that? To WHY did you do it?" And their truth comes out, as does the measure of calm and understanding she exhibits when she helps them find another way to behave.

She always makes the kids apologize to each other.

It is so important to teach children at an early age that sincerely saying "I'm sorry," can fix a world of hurts.

And then I laugh as she's telling it, and add.. "At least you didn't make them hug each other, like I did you and Chris. And like Mother did to Diane and me."

That was the worst. Having to hug your sibling when you're still busy being mad. LOL

So, today...I challenge all of you...even if it's just for today, to follow Kathy's lead and stop the bickering. Take the time to step out of an argument long enough to say "I'm sorry," and see what happens.

And if the urge hits you, hug them when you say it. Even they're still mad at the moment, what they'll remember later is the sincerity in your voice, and the hug from someone they love.

Said with love.

Sent with love.

I'm going to get a massage this morning. I am going to lie on that table and let go of every sad, every stress trigger, every concern, every troubled thought I've had this month.

Today I am going to give up the fight long enough to be relieved of the emotional weight I've been carrying.

And it will be my blessing for the day.

Love is how we identify our feelings toward another, and I'm not necessarily referring to emotional love. I mean...recognizing another human being as one of God's children. Seeing them through His eyes. Accepting that they aren't perfect, but then neither are we.

Sometimes I think we disagree most with the people who are the most like us. But it's because they mirror back to us our own flaws. And if we aren't ready to accept ourselves and our personal and emotional hang-ups, then we act it out upon them. It's like breaking a mirror and expecting not to see your own image again...and yet there you are... looking into someone else's face, into their lives, into their failures, and fears and seeing ourselves.

We can't hide from our own truths.

We can't pretend it didn't happen if you deny you are wrong.

And yet we do, time and time again, and that's how relationships fail, friendships are lost, and the love we should have had for the humanity in others becomes buried beneath what we don't want to admit.

Romantic, emotional Love happens when we're most ready to share a piece of our time and ourselves with another.

But that kind of Love can also deceive.

What you think is love, can be someone else's con.

Some people feed on the desperate need others have to be loved.

You can be lied to through love and never know it until it's too late.

You can see true love when there is none, through your own perceptions of needing to be seen as a person who matters.

These are the times when you can be hurt the most.

Don't give your heart away too soon.

Wait. Their own truths will out them soon enough.

Don't be so blind that they drown you in their own fight for survival.

Be wise in all matters of the heart.

Said with love.

Sent with love.

&.

Today.

I wrote one post early this morning and posted it, and then deleted it about 5 minutes later because it didn't feel right.

I have gone about my day, knowing when it mattered, the words would come. And they did.

In the grand scheme of life, some things matter more than others.

For a woman, her home is a reflection of her...and her life. She decorates according to what pleases her, with reminders and mementos of events and people who are special to her.

Coming home should be the place where she breathes a big sigh of relief and then lets go of every troublesome, hectic thing that happened during her day.

A man considered his home his castle.

A woman's home is her nest...a place of safety...like crawling into the back of a big deep cave and knowing she is sheltered and hidden for the time that she is there, unless she chooses to stand in the doorway and welcome others inside.

It is hers.... Except for the times when it is not.

Except for the times when illness or death invades her space.

When people she loves and shelters there are impacted by things that happen to them that are beyond anyone's control.

So with every ounce of strength, and every breath in her body, she abandons the care of home to care for people who cannot care for themselves.

One day of things out of order is normal...even a whole week with things piling up is not unusual in circumstances such as this.

But what if the care and healing of her loved ones requires darkness, no noise, no vacuums running, no music playing, no laughter-only whispers, and laundry piles up because the sound of machines becomes her patient's nemesis.

And that one week passes...and she can no longer go to work because she's carrying for her patient's needs, which include trips to doctors of every ilk.

Everything in her life ground to a halt in an effort to keep her patient alive.

She's lost her joy. She's losing strength daily because the simple act of falling asleep can mean trouble.

And when the unthinkable happens and one of her children is struck down by the same unbelievable injury...and begins suffering the same symptoms, her house is no longer her shelter, her safe place to be. It is part of the chaos within her life. In every room. At every turn. The reminders of what's been left undone only adds to the devastation of knowing everything she does, is still not enough.

After a heavenly intervention, one patient is no longer her total responsibility. Help came. And as they say, there's always tomorrow.

And tomorrow, some of her sisters of the heart are coming to her. We heard her plea. We're heeding the call. We're going to her home...her nest...and we're going to dust and mop and run vacuums, and washing machines and dryers, and fill her home with laughter as we do it.

Because as women, we understand that it won't just be cleaning her things...it will be cleaning away the bad memories, and the sad memories, and cleaning away the things that nearly broke her. The sound of our laughter will chase away the echoes of the past that swept through her life, and replace it with the power of the women who are part of her tribe.

And when we're done, we'll bless the house and all who dwell there. And when we're gone, the echoes she will hear will be laughter, and the things she sees will be her things, back where she first put them when she made the house her home, and it will be good.

All you have to do girl, is open the door, and direct the traffic.

We've got your back.

ॐ

Once upon a time I gave my sovereignty away.

Once I let a loud voice bury my own voice.

Once I gave up me for the sake of peace, thinking that would be the way to keep a happy home.

But what I discovered over time was that the more I conceded, the smaller my boundaries became.

I gave up all that was mine by birthright, and lost my inner light...my inner voice.

Time brings wisdom, and a growing intolerance with things that don't resonate. I was no longer willing to stay silent about things that did not reflect who I really was.

It caused conflict, but I was ready to reclaim me, and if it caused a war, so be it.

You can't grow, if you're not willing to adapt to change.

It can be frightening, but there's that 'leap of faith' they talk about.

It's real.

And I leaped.

So here I am. Standing in my own truth. Speaking what comes from my heart. Sharing what I know. What I have lived. What is possible if you are willing to leap.

My story is but one of millions.

But it's MY story, and that's what matters.

My identity is not linked to another.

I was first created from a spark of the light of the great I AM.

I came to Earth as someone's child.

I grew up as someone's sister.

I became someone's niece and someone's cousin.

I became someone's wife.

Then I became someone's mother.

Then someone's grandmother.

We aren't born to be identified by an attachment to someone else, no matter how precious that attachment is to us.

We cannot fulfill our soul purpose, if we cannot first find ourselves.

Balance is necessary before you can take the next step.

You knew that when you were learning to walk.

Nothing about that has changed.

Remember you have two feet of your own upon which to stand.

Find your balance and you will find yourself.

Said with love.

Sent with love.

৯

The message was strong this morning.

It was already in my head before I got out of bed. All I know is I'm supposed to TELL YOU. TELL YOU. TELL YOU.

And I'll be honest. I didn't want to write this. It's stuff I've known about for a long time, but it's also things I don't talk about, because so many people aren't ready to hear it.

And that's okay. If you aren't ready...then this message is not for you.

It is immaterial whether you believe this or not. It is not necessary to debate it. It warrants no personal arguments. If you don't like what I'm saying, have yourself a talk with God, not me. If you don't believe any of this is possible, then roll your eyes and move along.

I am just a messenger.

And this is the message:

All of the sad stuff, the scary stuff, the bad stuff that's happening now is an effort from the dark side to keep us afraid. To keep us herded into their corner. To make us believe that they, and only they are the ones who could possibly save us.

That's a lie.

And It's all part of the Shift.

The dark side is trying, with hate and with every evil thing they can do, to keep us divided. To make us hate each other. To make us afraid of each other.

They're losing their power and this is how it evolves for us.

New Earth has shifted into an energy that old Earth cannot survive in. The people in power...the people who were the followers...their truth has become impossible to hide. The darkness within each of them is visible now in how they behave, and the carnage they are causing.

Their glass towers are crumbling.

Accidents aren't always accidents.

What we're being told in the media is still the spin from the old power.

People who can't see this now...won't see it in this lifetime.

And it's okay. It's how it is playing out.

We're right where we need to be--in the God-light.

Standing up for right. Fighting against injustice.

Making a difference. Healing hearts. Asking for forgiveness.

Doing what's right by God.

Shunning the false ones. Stepping away from the hate.

Just know that you're okay. You are on your path. Don't panic by what you see and what you read and what you fear.

You're already living in New Earth.

Choose to stay there.

Choose the calm heart.

Choose the faithful heart.

Choose love.

Said with love.

Sent with love.

&.

Went to get some boxes to mail more books

Then I stopped at Walmart to get some fleece-style sweatshirts. I have exactly two tops that are warm enough for everyday winter wear. Everything else is lightweight. So now I have three more tops and two flannel shirts. $8.00 apiece and grateful I had the money to buy them. Now I just need to get them washed so I can wear them. Supposed to have a hard freeze tonight and possibly snow tomorrow.

Winter is knocking at the door.

I went by Panera Bread to pick up a little lunch to take home. My choices were total fails, but now I know not to order them again. Mediterranean quinoa salad and autumn squash soup.

Salad was not to my taste at all. Olives so salty that made my teeth hurt, dressing mostly lemon and oil, Lord love a duck! Talk about squinchy-face sour, and the soup was sweet. In my world, soup is not sweet.

Melted ice cream soup is, however, well received, if anybody asks.

I'm having a sad day, but it will pass.

It's just me having to come to grips with some changes.

It's not the end of the world.

Shit has been happening for eons.

People have disappointed other people for thousands of years and life still went on. So it will be now, as well.

I won't let life get me down, and neither should you.

Remember, we are steering our own ships.

If I don't like where it's going, all I have to do is turn the wheel.

I thanked God last night for healing those in need.

I thanked God last night for giving strength to those in need.

I thanked God last night for the peace and grace he gives to those in need.

I thanked God last night for the light He shines for those in need.

I thanked God last night for His presence in my life.

I do this every night.

So if you are in need of healing, or strength, or peace and grace in your life, or a little more light...I got your back.

Said with love.

Sent with love.

❦

One weird thing about social media.

It is an immediate way to get news out. We're all willing to share news. But we're really bad at updating ourselves. The update is ALWAYS posted on a news event, but no one seems inclined to click on a picture to look for an update.

It's also a symptom of how we've begun to receive information.

Ten second sound bytes.

A photo and a news blurb.

Very few people wait to hear the whole story.

They don't take the time to "read more".

Just click and share, click and share.

So it goes on and on and on forever.

Kind of like the old game we used to play when we were kids.

It was called Gossip.

We'd get in a circle, then whisper one thing really fast in the ear of the person to your right, then they'd whisper what they heard the same to the person next to them. When the last person in the circle got the 'news', she said it aloud.

Then the Gossip...the one who started the story, said aloud what it began with. The end results were always hysterical to us and it was never the same story as the one that began.

So this is kinda how sharing news runs on social media. One person starts a story, and maybe there is more added later to the story, and then there is always an update, good or bad, when people are found.

But imagine how those families feel when they keep seeing the faces of their loved ones shown over and over and over on social media, even after their crisis has ended, even when the crisis ended with a death.

On Social Media...the missing are never found, because no one bothers to check the story first.

It must be torture for the families.

Kindness means that whatever you say or do does not hurt or impact anyone. Not even in jest.

Gratitude means being so thankful for the thoughtfulness of others.

Love is an all encompassing feeling of good, joy, and happiness.

None of those cause harm.

All they cost you is that moment in time, when you pause to think before you speak.

§.

While the sunrise wakens me to a day of purpose, sunset always calls me home.

Like a mother, standing out on her porch calling the children in from play, I always heed the call with relief.

It's the time to pull shades, to unfasten the draperies to cover up the windows as I den myself up for the night.

Lights come on as I bring the day of purpose to an end in whatever way suits me best.

I feed my body, according to what I used up in that day.

If there was stress or tension, I seek quiet.

If there was grief, I shed tears.

If there was joy, I say a quiet pray of thanksgiving.

If there was disappointment, I set it aside, knowing something better is always waiting.

If there was anger, I release the residue and smudge it away.

I control my own space by who I let in to it, and I hold my sovereignty as a birthright.

We are not born to be other people's minions.

Because we are ALL parts of the God-light, we are valued, blessed, and loved.

And so on this night, after a day of mixed emotions, I have gone to ground, seeking quiet and peace.

Tomorrow will be a whole new day of purpose, but tonight is for tying up loose ends, fastening buttons, zipping zippers, and discarding that which is not pertinent to my life.

Don't let your day end without making peace with it.

That way, you do not begin a new one walking on crumbs from the past.

Sweep them up. Sweep them out.

Rest yourself in the knowledge that you are surrounded by angels.

Loved beyond measure from The One Most High.

And worthy of it all.

Said with love.

Sent with love.

&.

Every day, in some way, people are rising from the disaster that has befallen them, and looking for the way to move forward.

It is part of the self-preservation we are born with.

The reason we yank our hand back from the fire before we are burned.

The reason we don't go in water over our heads if we cannot swim.

The reason we distrust certain people upon meeting them.

It's part of our innate instinct--to move away from that which spells danger.

A Phoenix rising from the ashes of grief/disaster is a symbol for a new way of life.

You don't need a global disaster, or an act of weather, or the conflagration of massive wildfires, or explosions. to have the world as YOU knew it wiped out.

The end of one thing is always the beginning of another, because life is everlasting, and always comes full circle.

There are days when you can't see a way out of what's happening, but it's there.

Some days you get a sign.

Some days you're not ready to see it.

But when you do finally see it, the relief that comes to you then is a verification that your prayers were heard, and that you do matter. All of us matter.

We are all God-light, never to be dimmed.

The day after my Little Mama's passing, I saw this figure in the clouds, flying low above the ground.

A Phoenix, the long neck and head upright and looking forward, massive wings outspread, the long tail feathered out behind, like the trailing tail of a kite.

I saw the symbolism immediately. Her soul completing this life cycle, freeing both of us to move forward.

We are not born to become trapped in grief by someone else's passing.

Yes, we grieve, we remember them, we love them, but we must move past 'that day' to fulfill our purpose, too.

Said with love.

Sent with love.

We all have friends who say things that seem harsh to us, but maybe not to them.

They see the world from their own life and perspective, and that's how life is supposed to be.

But we all have an instinctive warning system that also says, move away.

A break in the relationship might happen when that friend finds something funny that horrifies you all the way to the bone.

It's like watching someone slap a child, or kick a dog. Or make fun of someone who's handicapped...or laugh at a homeless person. You know...the one thing that will never be okay with you?

So that happened to me yesterday.

I read the words, and then I felt the words, and when I did, it was like a door opened in front of me and I saw their truth. And I could not move away fast enough.

It wasn't a judgment in any way. That person is on their path, learning what they're here to learn.

But I knew in that moment her path was going one way, and mine is going another.

It's how friendships come and go. Sometimes we outgrow the friendships...not physically, but emotionally.

Some people are stuck in the past, repeating the same mistakes over and over and over. They don't move forward, because what they know is comfortable. They don't like it, but they are afraid of change. So they choose the devil they know, rather than the future they don't.

And in doing so, they can also become immune to compassion, and use their anger about their own life to decimate others.

They are their own worst enemy.

They poison themselves daily with what they say and how they think.

They are standing in shadows.

Other people experience the same thing, learn from it, and move past it. They might be anxious about the future, not knowing what will happen, but what they know for sure is that they don't ever want to repeat that mistake again.

They use their mistakes as a stepping stone to understanding.

Their words are tempered with kindness, they have learned that tears shed for others, are just as healing as the tears they shed for themselves.

They are standing in the light.

Friends are wonderful. Sometimes we are closer to our friends than to our own families.

But we do not owe an everlasting friendship to someone we no longer understand.

It is okay to feel like you no longer fit in their world, and it is okay for them to feel the same way about you.

We don't owe anyone a life-time of allegiance.

Honor your instincts.

Listen to your heart.

And if it doesn't feel right,

Step away.

Said with love.

Sent with love.

❧

Today is what you make of it.

Leave your personal baggage at home as you go to work, and leave your work baggage behind when you go home.

Look forward to one thing today, even if it's just lunch.

Silently bless the first person who smiles at you this morning.

And remember to smile at others you see.

You have two choices, both of which come from free will.

You can be satisfied with what you have.

Or envious of others because of what they have.

The first choice will change your life.

The second choice will ensure that your life never changes.

Holiday seasons approach.

There are several holidays that happen during this month, only one of which is Christmas.

This is America.

All kinds and colors of people with all kinds of lifestyles and religions live here.

There is no autonomy on religion.

Practice yours with kindness and love toward others.

A prayer is always answered.

It might not be the answer you wanted,

But it is the answer.

Love matters.

Practice it daily.

Said with love.

Sent with love.

❧

My version of happy may not be your version of happy.

My joys may come in different ways than the joys other experience. And that's okay.

All we have to do to get along and live in harmony, is allow each other the space to be who they are.

I know people develop understanding as they experience life.

But for some, what they learned made them afraid.

And the response to fear comes out differently in different people.

Some rage and attack, thinking they must to survive.

Some retreat so far inside themselves that they live the rest of their life behind huge emotional walls.

And some come out true survivors. It has changed who they were, but they're stronger for it, because they see themselves as having conquered that which almost brought them down.

Day before yesterday, I saw a couple walking, and pushing an older woman in a wheelchair. bundled up as best they could be against the cold. They carried everything they owned on their backs. And my heart broke. I wanted to fix it. I imagined what I could do if I had the money to make things like this go away.

But at the same time, I also understand their paths are different from mine. They were honoring soul contracts that were meant to help them learn or teach what they'd come here to do.

I never see street people as failures. I see survivors. I see people who don't quit. It doesn't change me wanting to save them, to at least make sure they have shelter and food, but I've accepted that my path and their paths were never meant to cross. I am an observer to their lives, but I am not a participant.

Like always, I ask God to bless them. Like always, the sight of their distress still breaks my heart. And like always, if someone is holding up a sign asking for help, I'll give them what I can, because I could not live with myself if I didn't. But accepting what belongs to me, and what doesn't belong to me, is part of understanding how life works.

We don't go where we're not wanted.

It is not our business to intrude into other people's chosen ways of life. When it is time, they bring about their own change.

Said with love.

Sent with love.

৯৯

Things I never take for granted in the winter:

How soft and warm my flannel sheets are when I jump in bed at night. It's as close to the feeling of being a kid again, as I have ever experienced as I remember the old cold farmhouse in which I grew up, and the rough wooden floors beneath my feet, right before I crawled into my little bed with the old flannel sheets.

The roof over my head and the comfort of food and warm clothes.

The errands my daughter and her family run for me so I don't have to get out when the streets are slick with snow or ice.

Memories that wrap around me like a blanket to comfort the ache in my heart during the long quiet nights.

Having a car.

Knowing how to cook food that warms and comforts.

The friends I have on FB, who share their lives with me, as I share mine with them.

Winter is for renewal. When we shed the shell of the past year, readying us for the next step in our journey, without the burden of what was...looking forward to what is...and what will be.

Said with love.

Send with love.

ه

I was bothered by something that happened this evening, so I went in the kitchen and made biscuits.

I can't describe how therapeutic it is for me to bake.

First, is to always turn on the stove and set the temperature.

Then it's getting down the old bowl I've been using since my kids were babies, getting out the ingredients, and the measuring cups, and quietly working, without television on, without any sound whatsoever but the occasional clink of a spoon to the bowl.

Turning the dough out onto the bread board, pushing it together without kneading, patting it out to the desired thickness, and using my old biscuit cutter rather than any of the four or five others that I have, because the biscuits just taste better with the old one. I promise.

There is such satisfaction in seeing those unbaked biscuits on the baking sheet as you slide them into the oven, and even more satisfaction when they come out, perfectly risen, and golden brown.

Baking is for the soul....truly, soul food at its most basic.

Yes, they tasted amazing.

They aren't really on my recommended food list.

But making them is high on my to-do list of what takes away the blues.

Stir up your own bit of magic by doing something that gives you joy...or gives you peace.

It's better than anything money can buy.

Said with love.

Sent with love.

ه

Some people have based their adult lives on being victims.

Even though they are grown, in their minds, they are still the orphan, or the person who goes often to the cemetery to 'visit' the dead partner, or the person who can't get ahead and blames it on everything but the free will of their own choices.

They look for other people to fill them up, and when those people fail them, they blame their misery on the people who let them down, instead of understanding that they are the only ones who can fix what's broken.

There are countless other examples of this, but the bottom line is, if they're looking back, they miss what's waiting for them ahead.

They can't heal, because they don't look forward.

They don't see a future.

They don't know how to see that.

They don't even know what it looks like.

It's easier to be the person they were, because they've already lived it, so they know how that goes, and when they do try something else and it doesn't turn out like they expected, then they just blame their failure on being the victim of their past.

It's far more difficult to be the person who's trying new things.

It's even scary not knowing how something is going to turn out, or what might happen if......

Their lives are in ruts so deep they can't see over them.

I know people like this.

I've felt like this myself a few times in my life.

But I had enough survivor instinct to see how toxic that kind of thinking can be.

What I know for sure is that when I stopped thinking about myself, and began helping others, is when life began to change.

If you see yourself in these words, know that you aren't alone.

All you have to do is make one small change in your life, in your routine, once a day, even if it's nothing more than taking a different road home.

Or trying one new food now and then.

Or moving the furniture around in your house.

Wear your hair a different way.

Clean your house.

Clean your car.

Don't live in chaos.

Don't live in the dark.

When you are no longer surrounded by disorder, then it's easier to feel the broken part of you. It's easier to realize, it wasn't where you lived. It wasn't how you looked.

You didn't realize that all you had to do was open the windows of your world, and let in the light.

Said with love.

Sent with love.

⁊♠

Just put Apple Praline Bread in the oven about fifteen minutes ago, and some baked apples in a dish beside it. My house smells soooo good.

Sending love today.

There are so many people in various stages of fear and grief.

I've been trying to finish up the paperwork on tying up the loose ends of Little Mama's life, but it's one thing after another, waiting for answers or copies of something, or waiting for other paperwork I need. I'm still waiting for death certificates, so until they arrive, everything comes to a halt.

And such is life.

I don't really have the Christmas shopping spirit this year. My left foot still hurts, so walking around stores in the mall is out, and I don't really care.

Everyone is getting a little money from me and that will be that. I doubt I'll make much candy, either. There are several people who won't be here, so I'll just scale back on dinner, too, and be better off for it.

I honor everyone's life choices, but at the same time, they know full well that means they have to honor mine...which means their drama is not my drama.

My house. My rules.

I live in a house of peace. :)

Happiness is a choice.

I choose it.

Said with love.

Sent with love

❧

It is not God's job to fix us when things go wrong.

God doesn't have a job.

He is The Creator, not the mechanic.

He gave us free will and freedom of choice.

If you're in a bind, it's because you put yourself there by choices you made, some of which may have been years ago, but the ripple effect is real.

One wrong step, one mistake never acknowledged is what builds despair and frustration.

Frustration leads to anger, and once you've hit rage, you're on your own.

You can pray to God for strength. But He'll likely just remind you that what you need is faith, and a change of lifestyle.

The power to fix your problems lies within you.

Don't blame others because you can't feel God.

It's not the job of the population on this earth to repair your road.

You're the one who left the ruts.

You're the one who looked away when things needed to be repaired.

If there are potholes in your road, fill them in, smooth them out, and move forward without drama.

You don't need praise for fixing what you broke.

You need to focus on what matters to you and proceed with caution, so that the next time you come up to a roadblock, you don't take everyone you love down with you.

Said with love.

Sent with love.

❧

I'm going to brave the mall today, but Kathy's going with me and I'm taking my wheelie...that's what I call the walker with wheels and a seat. Don't know how long I'll last, but I'll never know unless I try, and God and Bobby both know I don't quit.

I might not buy presents, but I still like to do stockings for my kids and grandkids so I need some little things for that.

Julia Fairbanks, I'm trying out that fudge recipe you recently posted. It's cooling now. Hope it's good, because it sure was easy. I'll let you know the family verdict. :)

It's really, really cold out today. The sun is finally shining, but the wind chill is pretty sharp, so I dressed for warmth, not fashion. As if I ever got in a snit about fashion, anyway. Too many years dressing for farm work to worry much about style.

Sending love and healing to all in need.

I continue to set aside anything that does not feel right to me, and I choose not to dwell upon anything happening in my family life that does not pertain to me and my house.

Everything is good beneath my roof, and I intend for it to stay that way.

That is a choice--my choice.

And for all of you, every day that you are unhappy where you are, it is because you have made the choice to stay there.

Even if you don't like where you are, or what's happening, by doing nothing about it, you chose to stay.

Said with love.

Sent with love.

※

I see my path clearest in the silence around me.

Messages come within the quiet rooms of my house.

Silence:

Once Mother Earth was alive with the sounds of life, but in many places, those sounds are gone. Habitats have been destroyed, paved over, and manufacturing and housing now stands where the copse of willows once grew. Where the cougar brought her cubs down to the spring to drink. Where the eagles flew highest.

Where the wolves ran at night. Where the buffalo roamed in great herds, spilling over valleys and hillsides in fluid unison.

It was simple then to hear messages from the Universe--to heed the warnings of Mother Earth. But her voice is smaller now, drowned out by noise pollution. And she is sicker now, poisoned by the pollution of man.

It is troubling to me, a child of the land, to not be able to find silence anymore, unless I am locked within the walls of my home. And even there, quiet is often disturbed by the sounds of sirens, or the constant roar of planes over my house from the flight path of the air force base.

When life has wounded you in any way, whether it be by disease or fate, silence, as the old saying goes, is truly golden.

People always say fevers get higher at night, or when they're sick, they begin to feel worse at night around bedtime.

But the truth is, it isn't night that brings how bad they feel to the forefront. It's the silence.

When the toys of civilization have been turned off, only then do you truly feel your body's pain. Only then does the fever and the sickness become real. Without distraction, you can attend to your needs in a timely manner.

Some people are afraid of silence. They don't want to think about their situation. They have used noise and people and social situations to distract them from whatever needs they have in their lives that are waiting to be addressed.

People go to church to hear someone else read the word of God to them, to interpret the meanings for them, to tell them how they should be living their lives.

But when you learn to be quiet, you are with God, and you already know.

Said with love.

Sent with love.

❧

I'LL RIDE IT OUT:

This is a phrase we use in this part of the country that means 'hanging on', regardless of what life is throwing at us.

We 'cowboy up' when the going gets tough.

We don't quit.

We don't back down.

The end result might not be what we wanted, but there is satisfaction in knowing you didn't let a situation destroy you.

That's really all that's asked of us in life.

To weather the complications with as much grace and dignity as we do the celebrations.

And NO, it isn't easy. But it's worth it.

It's like the time when my daughter was still in her teens, and fought off an attacker who broke into her home and came at her with a butcher knife.

She not only came out of the fight without a scratch, but she took the knife away from him. Blood flew then, and it wasn't hers, as she chased him out of the house. .

Yes, she was terrified. Yes, she suffered day and night terrors for years. And yes, she's still leery. But she didn't let that destroy her. She is one of the few people who already know how they'll act in moments of danger, or in life-threatening situations.

She didn't let herself become the victim.

And that's what I mean.

Life doesn't always thrust you into mortal danger, but whatever the trouble, don't throw your hands up and quit. Don't wait for someone else to save you.

Figure it out.

Solutions.

They're how you solve problems.

Pick one and move on, because the longer you wait, the bigger the issue becomes in your mind.

The problem hasn't changed...it's just sitting there...but by not solving it and moving on...the problem changes you.

Said with love.

Sent with love.

❧

So...Spirit woke me up just after 5:00 A.M.

I tried and tried to go back to sleep, but finally gave up, got dressed and here I am delivering the message.

You are not in a funk--in limbo--uncertain--confused--lost.

You are just missing the point of where you are at this time.

The down times in our lives are for growth. This is when your soul light is trying so hard to shine through the shadows you've let into your world, to let you know this is your reprieve.

This is when you've come through an experience that has used up all of your emotional energy, and it is time to replenish.

I know it's hard to come down from drama.

It can become the drug in your life. You don't know how to move through life without someone else's energy draining your spirit.

But here's the thing.

When you only know how to REact, then you have lost the ability to ACT on your own.

Maybe this event has finally come to an end, and you're going through your days angry with someone else, when the truth is, you put yourself in it, and now that you're out of it, you have to learn how to live with YOU.

You are no longer the wall that is reverberating someone else's life.

What you call being in a funk, or confused about what to do, or where to go next, is actually you, ignoring the fact that you have your own purpose, and you aren't supposed to need a partner to make it happen.

When it comes to soul work, you do that on your own.

This is your time to grow and heal.

Said with love.

Sent with love.

❧

The more people comment about other people's appearances, the more they reveal about themselves.

Cruelty is hidden behind laughter.

Snobbery is revealed by comments.

Envy rings.

This behavior does not depict someone with wit.

It is the behavior of insecurity and jealousy, of anger and rage.

Stating that you don't care what anyone thinks -

That you are proud of saying what you think is a defense mechanism.

What they do not understand is that they become that of which they speak.

They are living and breathing within the aura of shaming others,

And then wonder why their lives never go as planned,

Why nothing good ever happens for them.

If one day, those same people dared to step out of their habit and began saying upbeat, positive things to people, and stopped sharing hate and discord, they would be shocked at how quickly their own lives changed with it.

You want to be happy?

It comes from within you.

No one can give it to you.

It's learned behavior.

Stand within the space of kindness and humanity and you open yourself up to a different way of life.

Said with love.

Sent with love.

❧

Today is a day for the healing of hearts, souls, and bodies.

I have said prayers for all of you.

Regardless of your needs, I have prayed for them to be met.

The answers come in their own fashion, according to soul contracts and soul requests, regardless of what loved ones are asking for you.

Be kind to yourself.

Be thoughtful of others.

Walk the peaceful path, so that the only signs of your passing are the footsteps you leave behind.

Said with love.

Sent with love.

§.

Yesterday I hugged a perfect stranger because she was crying.

Today I got a perm.

Tonight I gave away the last of my banana nut bread.

Tomorrow I have to go pick up death certificates.

I'm sure you think all of this is random and has no meaning together, but it does.

It is the perfect example of life.

At any given moment, what you're doing becomes less important than what you are witnessing.

Every day we pursue mundane tasks because someone has to.

When opportunities arise to share what you have with someone else, the joy you receive far outweighs the effort you spent making it.

And doing things you don't want to do is what being an adult is all about.

Life isn't meant to be easy or perfect.

But it is meant to be lived with every ounce of energy and joy you can put into it.

And when living it gets hard, and the sadness within you is so strong you're afraid to take a deep breath for fear of coming undone---

This is when you fall back on faith.

Not the kind of faith where you plan on God performing a miracle for you.

The kind of faith in knowing whatever you are going through, you're not doing it alone.

Remembering that you are an all-knowing soul and the power to rise above disaster is always within you.

You just have to have faith that your instincts will guide you to do the right thing.

At any given moment when you are at a breaking point, within the time it takes for your heart to beat you will surrounded by angels. They're your angels. They were assigned to you from the moment you took your first breath on Earth, and they are always within the sound of your voice.

They aren't meant to interfere with the choices you make, but if you can find a quiet place to be when you are at your lowest, you can feel their all-encompassing love.

They are the emotional cheerleaders you need as you find the strength to pull yourself together.

They are the wind at the back of your neck as you look out across a place that gives you peace -

The touch you thought you imagined.

The whisper in your ear that spurs you to take just one more step. They are our God-link to home.

And when all of the trouble has passed, and you have regained your sense of self, it is then you take note of what just happened, and give thanks that it is over and you're still here.

The point of hardship is remembering how you survived it, and learning never to repeat what started it.

Said with love.

Sent with love.

❦

It's thundering and raining here this morning. I've already been out in it and am home. Scout came over just a bit ago, but he radiates so much energy that I will still feel his presence for quite a while after he's gone.

#Oldsoul....#confidantofhispath..

I love that's who he is.

Yesterday was a hard, sad day for many, and today will be the letdown for others who spent yesterday with families in celebration of the holiday.

It is the Yin and Yang of life. Sometimes we're up emotionally, and sometimes we're down, but it doesn't mean anything dire.

It's just us riding the ebb and flow of life.

As much as I dislike being around huge bodies of water, I see the way we live our lives mirrored with an ocean.

On the surface, we either see calm seas and sunshine, or whitecaps warning of things to come, or the thunderous crashing of massive waves against the shore.

We live life the same way. Good days, frustrating days, days that threaten to pull us under with grief or pain.

We see people who appear to have everything. But we can't see below the surface of what they present to the world--like the depths of an ocean...you cannot see what's beneath your feet.

Wishing to trade your life for another person's life is as risky as buying something sight unseen.

Be careful what you wish for.

People are already talking about the new year and making resolutions.

But why wait for a specific date when you know you already desire change?

Be proactive, but with care, because there is a codicil that comes with that suggestion.

If, in your desire to make changes in your life, you still hold responsibilities to others, then they always have to be part of the decision. If you choose to eliminate their opinions from what you're planning to do, then you HAVE to accept that you will encounter trouble. You can't have everything you want at the cost of other people's feelings. Not when you're abdicating your role as a parent, or a spouse, or a caregiver and there are underage children or people depending on you for physical care involved. Above all things, you never...ever...walk away from that without expecting the karma that brings.

Case in point: I always wanted to travel to Ireland...and to Alaska...and to Scotland. But when I had the money and the health to enjoy that, my mother needed me. And so I let go of that dream, because I loved her more than any dreams I might have had.

I now have the time, but I don't have the money or the desire to travel anymore, and I don't feel like I missed anything. The satisfaction of knowing I kept her safe and loved far outweighed any daydreams I might have had.

It's about doing what's right.

So, if you want to change your life and your responsibilities weigh you down, then change your attitude about where you are in life, and know that as long as you draw breath, your future is always open.

Said with love.

Sent with love.

ᆥ

Why is it so difficult for people to understand that we're not supposed to be alike?

The most special part in each of us is the part that makes us different from everyone else.

Some people refer to that trait as being unique.

Some 'unique' people are loners.

Some have been disenfranchised from their families because they see life from a different point of view.

Some have even found a way to market their differences successfully.

But it's more common for being different to cause fear, and when people are afraid, they make mistakes, sometimes terrible mistakes. They use anger as their weapon, and lash out with unforgivable words, or with their fists, putting scars on more than the body they pummel.

Scars on the heart leave memories that, thru the years, become nightmares that change who people are meant to be.

Some people claim they're acting on behalf of their particular religion, demanding that everyone believe as they believe. But there is only one God, known to all by many names.

And that one God only asks one thing of all of us.... "To do unto others, as you would have them do unto you."

When you use the name of God to shame someone you see as different, you shame yourself instead.

This world is a 5D world, a world that operates within the 5D energy of love.

There is no place here for religious persecution or racial prejudice.

There is no place here for ignoring those in need of basic human care.

We were born of God-light, a spark from the one and only great I Am.

It is time to remember where we came from.

It is time to end discord--to live and let live.

Said with love.

Sent with love.

❧

When we're fighting via social media, deceit in high places goes on right under our noses. Don't buy into the ridiculous. Don't pass around inflammatory stories or Memes that you don't even know are really true. Just because someone put a political Meme in a little box with a colorful background does not mean it is valid. A few clicks on Google to check for facts is all it takes to recognize that you are being played.

Why start a brand new year with the same old stories?

That bubble you're choosing to live in is going to pop, and when it does, you will blame everyone else for what is going to amount to your inattention to the truth.

When I was a child, New Year's Eve meant nothing to me except that I got to write a different year on my school papers when I turned them in. I remember when we went from 1949 to 1950 because that was the year I stated school. I was six years old.

When I was a teenager, New Year's Eve was a source of anxiety. IF I even got to go to a party, I was worried I wouldn't have a boyfriend who would kiss me at midnight, and if I did have one, I was still worried he might kiss me at midnight. LOL

When I was a young married woman I went to parties and everyone got drunk but me. Have you ever been the only sober person at the entire event?

When I had children, I didn't want to ever leave home on New Year's Eve. I didn't want to be the statistic and leave my kids orphans because of some drunk driver.

The last New Year's Eve I celebrated was with Bobby, but not with liquor. It was love that took us into the New Year. I didn't know then it would be our last one together.

These days I am happily alone on New Year's Eve, and when the countdown begins, I sit with my memories of the people I have loved and lost, knowing that as every tomorrow comes, anything is possible

Said with love.

Sent with love.

§♣

Starting the New Year off on a positive note.

Yes, there is a lot of turmoil and sadness in the world, but there is also a lot of good...

Miracles are happening every day.

People are surviving and thriving.

Some have gone through devastating heartbreak but they are walking out of it stronger for the lesson.

Where some people see failure, others are seeing hope.

Where some quit in frustration, others keep putting one foot in front of the other and move through the roadblock they had encountered.

Some don't ever look to see what's wrong.

They look to see what's right.

Where some continually focus on the darkness,

Others look first to the light.

There is nothing between you and happiness but your mindset.

There is no way you can be defeated unless you quit.

Understand it's never about being punished.

Look always for the lesson.

God doesn't punish anyone.

We punish ourselves with guilt and fear-based rage.

Accept the knowledge that life is always cycling. Sometimes we are in a cycle of plenty, and sometimes we are in a cycle of hardship.

Life is never barren.

But it can be in a state of hibernation.

When your spirit has been so wounded that you can't draw breath without pain, that's when the soul within you pulls you back, holds you close, let's you heal.

You came here with all the power and the knowledge of the Universe within you.

Trust your instinct.

Trust yourself.

Said with love.

Sent with love.

ॐ

Men and women are more alike than they are different.

Separated by sex due only by the kind and amount of hormones in their bodies, they both have brains that can think and reason.

They deserve to be treated fairly, and they deserve the same amount of consideration.

They both love, laugh, cry, and rage.

They are humans.

In the eyes of God, they are all pieces of Him.

Showing prejudice because of race, color, or religion is denouncing the Great I am.

Shaming others because you denounce their right to be who they are, is shaming the same God-light that is within you.

You do not have that right.

God did not give you that power.

For some of us, the only difference between night and day is the amount of light with which we can see in a twenty-four period of time.

But if only sunlight is used as a rule of thumb for how time is measured, then you have dismissed whole populated continents who's days and seasons must be measured by a clock and a calendar. In those lands and in certain seasons of the year, sunlight is often little more than a half-light, and darkness lasts for months, and that is their normal.

You cannot expound upon that which you have never seen. You cannot judge that which you do not understand.

No matter how well-traveled or well-read you are, your life experiences are still not enough to stand in judgment of another person's decisions.

Until you have lived it, you cannot understand it.

It's like trying to explain childbirth to a man.

Or a man trying to explain his own emotions.

If we do not stand in those shoes, our reactions and opinions are ours alone.

Criticism is not the same thing as a comment. One is a judgement. The other is an observation.

Live in peace.

Stand in truth.

Love one another.

Said with love.

Sent with love.

The first thing I see is light.

Always.

It's what I look toward first.

It's the first thing my eye is drawn to in a picture.

It brings still pictures and painting to life.

Light guides us.

We are full of light, and we can grow the light within us by our words and actions.

Darkness exists ONLY because it is the absence of light.

It isn't a bad thing. Some animals are nightwalkers.

They sleep in the day and live and hunt in the night.

Some plants thrive in shade.

And some plants only bloom at night.

It is the yin and yang of life.

Sometimes people are so full of darkness that they become a danger to themselves and others.

But their choices and actions have smothered the God-light with which they came, and they are on a personal path of destruction.

Those people and their troubles belong to God.

It is not our business to try and change them.

No one can exact change within another.

That is on the person who has become a nightwalker, too.

Say a prayer for them and move on.

I am a lightworker.

It is my path to walk in peace and kindness.

I am unhappy to be any other way, so I choose what is right for me.

I choose the gentle way.

I choose my friends with care.

I choose not to compromise my dignity or my beliefs.

I choose the path bathed in God-light.

I choose LOVE.

Said with love,

Sent with love.

Good morning, and how are all my sweet peeps today?

Me? I locked myself in my bedroom and couldn't get out.

Had a small Smith fit and then immediately calmed down, pointed to the doorknob and said aloud..."all right you guys....fix this!" and walked away.

I brushed my teeth, washed my hair, and dressed, then had already figured out how I could get out and back into the other part of the house when I walked back to the door, turned the knob once. I felt it slipping again, and then it caught and VOILA...I was out.

"Thank you," I said aloud, picturing Bobby and a band of angels frantically manipulating the inner workings of that faulty lock to save me...then went to call a locksmith, ONLY to find out the power had been out sometime in the night for over two hours, which meant I had phone service, but no way to look up the phone number except the cell phone..

Sooooo, I had to boot up the PC, then sat down to use my phone.

I said... "Okay Google," Google responds.."How can I help you?"

"I need a locksmith In.....(I named my town and state).

Miss Google comes back and asks me. "What do you need a lock-smith for?"

I stared at the phone a sec. Is Google serious? I answered. "A lock."

Silence.

I rolled my eyes and disconnected. Appears Google was having a morning something like me. I got up to see if my computer was up and running and it was. Found my locksmith guy and made the appoint-ment. All the while, I'm thinking, Google is just like the kid in class who holds up her hand EVERY time the teacher asks a question, and then when she is called on, doesn't have the answer. This isn't the first time she's lost her cool with me, so I've come to look upon Google as being about as much help as the neighbor down the street when I ask for directions.

He waves his arms and hands about with such abandon as he gives directions, that it looks like he's trying to land a plane. And, I quit asking him, because his directions are seriously flawed. LOLOLOL

At any rate, I have a locksmith coming later this afternoon.

I have had my Hunger Control Slim and am having my breakfast for lunch.

I think the lesson for me this morning was two-fold.

One was to remain calm, which I never do when appliances screw up.

And the other lesson was that I knew I had Bobby help, and I'd already figured a way out if he was on another job. LOL

I could just hear him saying, "Baby, I can fix that, you don't need to call a..."

But when we were still together, and he didn't immediately go to the job to do it, the minute he left the house to go tend to horses, or whatever was going on on the ranch, I called the plumber, or the elec-trician, or whoever I needed to fix it. He knew I had all the patience in the world with people, but absolutely none when appliances let me down.

So, he and my Guardians were on the job for me this morning and that's a win every time.

Trust your sources.

Don't be afraid to use them.

Jesus said, "Ask and ye shall receive."

I'm not afraid to ask.

You should not be either.

Said with love.

Sent with love.

&.

Neither your age or your appearance is any indication of what's in your heart.

You and only you know the secrets you came with.

You, and only you, have the inner compass that tells you when you're off course.

Understanding this is the first step in taking away anyone else's responsibility to how your life is, at any given time.

So many people live their lives as victims, blaming circumstance and other people's actions for why they are where they are.

You can say that.

You can claim their guilt as the explanation for why you view your life as failing.

BUT, if you are brave enough to write down everything thing you hate about your life, beginning with the earliest dates and continuing up to the present time, and then you start remembering what was going on in your life at that time, you will realize where the first wrong step was taken.

And you will see, as you continue through the dates all the way up to the present time, if you're honest with yourself, you will see, and you will remember, the times when you could have made another choice. A choice that would have taken you in a new, and different direction.

Everything that happens to us is a lesson if we survive it. And if we do, then that means we should have learned something from it. As we were going through the hard stuff, the thing most obvious to us should have been that this was something we never want to go through again.

Yet time and time again, people get out of one disaster, only to move forward, still raw and bleeding from the last situation, and choose NOT to change. Or...they make a change, but all of the energy and presence in which you've moved into is either the same or worse than where you were...and it's no one else's fault that you're there.

Listen to your conscience. It's your body's survival instinct. If you want a better way, then stop pointing fingers and naming everyone's name but your own.

You can lie to everyone you know.

But you can't lie to yourself and make it stick.

Said with love.

Sent with love.

🐚

How long does it take a heart to break?

A heartbeat, no more, no less.

The wrong thing carelessly said can cause irreparable damage to a relationship--to a friendship--to a lover--to a child.

The body is strong. A person's constitution can be rock solid.

But a hateful look or an angry word said to someone who loves you can never be taken back. And in those instances, there can be collateral damage to the witnesses.

One parent enraged by the other parent, begins calling them names, cursing, damning, publicly hating them, and the children absorb that fight as their fault, because 9 times out of 10, the fight is about them.

In those moments when you were out of control, you broke them. You forever changed who they were meant to be.

If a child hears a father say he hates his wife, then they hear that as they are being hated, too, because they are half of her.

If a child hears a mother tell her husband she wishes he was dead, or that he's worthless, then she has just given her child the same damning curse, because they are half of him.

Children are part of two people. Whether they are adopted, or the children you birthed, they have identified as belonging to a couple. But when the couple splits in acrimony, the children are also torn. Regardless of who they go to live with, they suffer from the ongoing battle of the sexes, and in the bitterness between the couple, they are witnesses to the death of a family.

It is completely selfish of adults to behave in such irresponsible manners. Once you have committed to being a parent, you are FOREVER a parent, no matter how old you are, or where life takes you.

You can't undo what's been said or done.

And unless you are adult enough to remember there are other people to be considered in the breakup of a relationship besides yourself, you will lose their trust. Forever.

They may hang on to the idea of a loving parent.

But they have lost the belief that they mattered to you.

And if that doesn't break YOUR heart, then you have none to break.

Said with love.

Sent with love.

$$\approx$$

We are born into a family and connected by proximity and blood.

We choose our friends, based on shared likes and lifestyles.

And then there is the group of people you know who feed your soul. They are your tribe. You are connected to each other almost instantly by soul recognition. You have shared reasons for being here...and you both had to cross paths to fulfill the soul contracts for which you came.

You aren't just friends on Earth.

You have been linked forever since the moment your tiny God-lights first winked.

Spending time with your tribe is how you feed your soul.

It raises energy, brings joy, settles worrisome thoughts, reminds you that you matter, and brings peace.

I'm spending time with a person from my tribe this afternoon.

The time spent together resets my inner clock.

Reminds me to shed that which is unimportant in the grand scheme of things, and to focus on the purpose for which I came.

A soul sister is that friend who holds your deepest secrets as if they were her own.

And what you understand as you journey through life with the tribe at your back is that while you know any of them would help you in a heartbeat, you have to realize that they expect the same thing of you.

Belonging to a tribe means unity...not just the gathering of spirit.

Treasure your tribe.

Said with love.

Sent with love.

§

The next two days are for discarding everything that is no longer of use to you.

Grudges. Nobody wants them.

Anger. It served no positive purpose in your life.

Jealousy. It is an emotion of immaturity.

Fear of failure. There's no such thing as failure. Just a lesson learned.

Let it all go.

Saving clothes that no longer fit is self-defeating.

All you're saying to yourself is that you aren't good enough the way you are.

Old emotional wounds and grief.

Sometimes when we lose a loved one, the only thing we have left of them are memories and grief.

And when the memories begin to fade, we hold onto the grief even longer and tighter as if we have to stay sad so that they're still a part of our lives.

Let them go.

What you don't understand is that when we become spirit again, the thing we want most is to see our loved ones happy. To see them thriving. To know they're not holding onto the past, so remember them with joy. That's how you honor a loved one who's gone.

Let go of all the rest. It no longer serves you.

Trying to be someone you're not.

You can't control the fact that some people will never like you.

All that means is that you crossed paths with someone who has no purpose in your life and no bearing on the path you walk.

Let them go.

Life changes coming.

The next two days in the Universe are crucial times in staying positive and being at peace with who you are.

The first full moon of a new year is called a wolf moon.

In some beliefs it's a blood moon.

Tonight all of the planets in our solar system will be aligned.

Tonight is a full lunar eclipse.

Any one of these alone would hold high vibrations of energy, but together, the aspects of these events are astronomical.

Release whatever negative emotions you hold.

The days of the 20th and the 21st are crucial times to stand in the light of peace and love and know that you are blessed.

Said with love,

Sent with love.

❧

I don't know what you guys were doing today, but I had a 90 minute massage this morning, ate lunch at Zio's at noon, went to Walmart and stocked up on groceries for the bad weather coming in this weekend, filled my car up with gas, and went to the bank.

It was almost three p.m. when I got home and I'm sitting with my feet up near the fire, drinking my ice tea and chilling out a bit before I get back to work on my current manuscript.

I liked this day.

I don't always look forward to what's on my daily agenda, but today rocked.

Yes, it was a treat to get a massage, but it was also very necessary to my well-being.

When you sit for hours on end working at a computer, the amount of muscle tension that turns into pain in my neck, back, and shoulders is miserable.

I am grateful.

Yes, I like going to Walmart.

I appreciate that I have the money to pay for my groceries. There have been times in my life when I lived on credit cards to be able to eat.

I appreciate that I have the money to fill my car up with gas, because there have been plenty of times in my life when $5.00 worth of gas was all I could manage. Yes, gas was a bit cheaper then, but it never filled up my car.

No, I don't mind eating alone. I've been eating alone at home for years. Eating alone in public is no different to me.

Every day brings a new set of challenges.

That's what life is about.

Some days it looks like a maze with no end in sight.

Some days it's all a trouble-free zone.

But most days it's a mixture of both.

I don't sit and dwell on what I've lost.

I think about what I've gained.

I don't meddle in anyone else's business.

I don't spread false information.

If I am offended by someone's words or behavior, I simply walk away.

Nowhere does it say I must comment.

This is how I maintain peace in my life.

I don't need the world to be perfect before I'm happy.

I choose happiness.

I choose Love.

❧

There are many good people in this country.

Some advocate for the protection of animals.

Some work to end homelessness.

Some work in free clinics, getting medical care for people who have none.

Some advocate for immigrants.

Some donate their time and money doing charity work on their own.

But what is needed is a population that sees all of this as worthy.

A population that would not pick and choose.

A population that would never question humanity as a world-wide issue.

What if it came to pass within the human race that if someone judged others by the color of their skin, that they would become color blind? That they began seeing everything...people and their surroundings, and everything they owned in a neutral color.

What if it came to pass within the human race that being mean to someone...harming them in any way, meant virtual exile? That you would become invisible to everyone around you?

What if it came to pass within the human race that lying to hurt someone meant the lie you told about them would become your reality?

What if it came to pass within the human race that physical violence against another, or taking someone's life, meant that the perpetrator would immediately feel the actual fear and pain of what they'd just done to someone else?

If there were known personal consequences for every moral or unlawful crime, then the slogan 'crime doesn't pay' would actually become a truth.

It is imperative to the collective conscience of us all to do better and be better than we ever were before.

There is opportunity now, in this higher level of energy on earth, to move upward into a place...a kind of dimension...where humanity has evolved beyond war and famine. Where people care as much about the earth on which they live, as they care about the people on it.

Step out, and step up.

All you have to do is LOVE one another.

Don't hesitate too long or you'll miss the ride.

Said with love.

Sent with love.

೬

Water is off on my block. The city has been working on it, digging up this giant hole in the street in front of the house next to me since around 2:00 p.m.

It's 5 hours later and still no water. It's dark out, and so cold, and they're still there working.

Sorry it's happening, but I sure hope they turn it back on soon.

I went out to eat supper tonight because of it. Went to Zoe's Kitchen and had vegetarian lentil soup and some hummus and pita bread. Came home with the hummus and pita I didn't eat.

Very sad coming home though. All the lights and the cars zipping up and down, and people in big warm coats coming in and out of businesses, and then you see the street people with their sleeping gear on their backs, just walking. I guess going to wherever they can find a safe place to sleep out of the wind.

This sight is one of the most troubling to me.

This, and people sick and dying and being turned away for medical care.

It is an abomination that this still exists in the world.

As I was driving to the restaurant I drove up on a red light. Then the light turned green, and yet there we sat in a long line of cars, waiting for that first goober at the front of the line to put down his dang phone and look up.

And all the people closest to him just sat there, as well. I guess they were on their own stupid phones. Finally, here's me, seven cars back, and I think enough is enough, and I lay on the horn.

All of a sudden, there's movement up front and off we go.

little. As I was driving, I kept remembering how horns were used when I was little.

People honked when they saw someone they knew, and waved as they were passing. They honked when they arrived at someone's house to let them know they were there so they'd come call of their dogs. They honked when they went out into the pasture to feed. Cows came running at the sound. And that was it.

As I grew older, and families began having multiple cars, and there was more traffic everywhere, people honked in frustration. And honked when they passed you so you would they were flipping you off. Locals in a town honked during a pep rally parade to let everyone know their team was going to a big game, or honked coming back into town to let everyone know they won.

Then as I grew older, honking was road rage, pure and simple.

Honking was either anger, or it was the boyfriend sitting out in his car, honking for his date to get her ass to the car. (That stuff never happened when I was growing up, because the only person coming out of the house would have been my Daddy, cussing a blue streak for their rude behavior.

Now, no one honks, because if there is a pause in traffic, no body looks up to see why. They're on their phones.

But, as long as there are people like me, who don't like to sit through two green lights because someone feels the need to read a text from a friend instead of tending to business, I will be blasting them from the back of the line, reminding them to either move forward, or get the heck out of my way.

This has been a day of learning and revelations for me.

I won't say why, because the reasons are all personal, but it reinforces why I keep saying..LOVE is the key.

Love yourself.

Love one another.

When you give yourself up to LOVE, everything else falls into place.

Love makes you happy.

Happy brings joy.

Joy brings more joy to you, and so it goes.

Love the broken...but don't try to fix them...they are on their own path, and maybe broken is what they came here to experience.

Pray for them. Show kindness. Feel LOVE toward them, but don't own their pain because it's not yours to feel.

Once you understand that you can no more take away someone's troubles for them, than you can take away their joy, then you understand the human experience for which you came.

Whatever they have...hardship or plenty, it's theirs.

Your own troubles and your own joys are for you to work through.

You don't pray to God to fix you, because He didn't break you.

You broke yourself, and it is your job to find a way through it.

It's what you came here to do...to learn.

Free will is the reason you are in a jam.

Free will is the only thing that will get you out.

Yes, God loves you as a Father loves a child, but you are NOT His puppet, to be manipulated here and there.

You are a strong and powerful spirit and the sooner you remember that, the sooner your life will change.

One way or the other, it will change.

It's up to you to make the right decisions.

Said with love.

Sent with love.

❧

You know that feeling you get when everything is going your way? Maybe it doesn't happen often enough to brag about, but when it does, what we get from those good feelings is like the leavening agent needed when you bake.

It has to be there for the bread to rise.

So if you're in need of joy, then lift yourself up.

The key to happiness is within you.

Think of yourself like a pot about to boil over. You're on the verge of losing it, and then someone tosses in a couple of ice cubes, or puts a lid on it, or stirs it down.

That's what laughter can do for your pain.

That's how powerful love is from the smile of a stranger.

So knowing that, why then, do you still choose the angry road?

The blaming road?

The road to Envy is a dead end.

The road to Joy is endless.

There is nothing...and I mean NOTHING that is stopping you from changing your attitude but you.

Getting a raise won't change the inner you.

Buying pretty things won't fix what's wrong in your heart.

Creating chaos within a family so that you are constantly the center of attention is a narcissistic trait.

It doesn't mean the chaos you cause is justified.

It just highlights your continuing need to be the victim.

However, if using your free will to create chaos is your choice, then so it is.

But understand, no one is required to be your audience.

Their choice to step out of your chaos is them using their free will.

The trouble with that soul contract you made with the dark side is in the fine print.

The day will come when you rage all alone.

Love yourself.

Love one another.

Be the peacemaker.

There's still time.

Said with love.

Sent with love.

ৡ

Take nothing for granted.

Temper your thoughts before you speak.

Trust yourself first.

Enough is all you need of anything.

Need is when something you don't have is critical to your health, life, or family.

No one needs an excess of anything.

Some people have an excess of everything,

But 'things' are neither a prerequisite or a necessity to reach inner peace.

Salt your conversation with words that perfectly season every moment of your life.

Appreciate.

Love.

Kindness.

Love.

Wonderful.

Love.

Generous.

Love.

Special.

Love.

Amazing.

Love.

Glorious.

Love.

Magnificent.

And Love.

Don't forget the LOVE.

Said with love.

Sent with love.

જ

Do you know why witnesses to a crime often make completely different statements as to what they saw?

It's because of their perception of facts.

Our perception of a truth is often based on our personal experiences and how we were raised.

If you only see the world in black and white, right and wrong, night and day...then you are missing the nuances that shades and colors add to life, as well as to what you see.

From the day we are born, parental prejudices and life experiences begin to shape the adults we will become.

If you grow up without being exposed to the beautiful differences we all share, without knowing it, you have been emotionally blinded and crippled.

It isn't your fault if you were raised that way, but if, as an adult, you finally see the colors, and the shadows, and you still reject the existence of their truth, then that fault is yours.

We use but a small portion of our brains, but think what we might become...what a magnificent human experience being born would be...if we expanded our perceptions and life experiences to include more than the tribe you belong to now...to include more than the clan you claim?

What if we saw ourselves in every person we met during a lifetime?

What if our meeting garnered immediate understanding of why and how they become who they are...and in turn...they immediately understood the why and how we became to be?

Having that ability would end wars.

Knowing why creates empathy.

Empathy creates love.

Love is the key that opens the door to a blanket understanding of all aspects of humanity.

Love is the medicine that heals.

Love is the answer.

Said with love.

Sent with love.

꿈

Being upset with someone who sees people in a different light is futile.

Don't rage. Don't take all that negativity you're feeling about someone else into your heart. You can't change them. They're on a different level of soul development and do not have the same perceptions you do. It doesn't make them stupid. It doesn't make them bad. They're here learning a lesson, too.

But the lesson they came to learn is one your soul learned long ago...in another lifetime...when you were on the same kind of journey...and the trust you put in the wrong people destroyed you.

Empathize for the lesson they will eventually learn, but don't hate on them. Don't give them a bigger reason to be defensive. Don't make them dig into perceptions they're trying to learn and cause them to fall farther away from truth.

If you feel the need to interfere...then pray for them. That's the kind of interference all of us need.

Let them be.

Said with love.

Sent with love.

§

Every person born into this world will experience all emotions of the spectrum and have life experiences that hurt them, broke them, or caused them great grief.

No one escapes this. It's part of life.

The trick is not to let that identify you.

Don't become your worst experience.

Don't get up and put on that mantle every day, as if you were putting on your clothes.

Don't identify yourself as 'that' person.

And by the same measure, we will also experience great joy and delight.

If great things are accomplished in your lifetime, in no way are you allowed to rise above the rules of society.

Success does not make you exempt from decency and honor.

If you don't know how to express what you feel the need to be...then live by example.

There is no need to decry you are the best at what you do.

Just be the best.

Your actions, and the accolades of others will say it for you.

We are not the worst. We are not the best.

We are not the homeliest. We are not the prettiest or the most handsome.

Save for cleanliness and grooming, We are how God made us, and we appear as we do through no actions of our own.

We are the sum total of a spark from the Great I Am.

Some lights burn brighter than others, because souls are always at work growing light.

The older your soul is, the greater the wisdom and the brighter the light.

Be as kind to the young souls, as you would your own children.

Have the wisdom to see and understand the differences of people without letting emotions cloud the way.

If some offend you, just walk away.

They are on a journey of their own.

And if you offend others, and are wise enough to know what you said and did was hurtful, it is upon you to make the peace.

Said with love.

Sent with love.

ی

At night, in my sleep, I fly. I run.

Unlimited by the bonds of body and earth, I am free.

It is the gift--the reminder of the soul I am--to be the human I am meant to be.

In this mindset, an aging body, physical restrictions, and a life alone are nothing for which I am concerned.

Life has seasons, like the earth.

And some lives extend, where others, (seen through human eyes) seem to have been cut short.

What I know as a soul is hard to remember in this life.

We are often held captive by repeated messages that death is a punishment.

And we mark the loss of a loved one because of age, or the accident, the disease, the act of violence, the suicide, the disappearance as the tragedy it is.

It is so hard to experience that kind of loss. For some, it is a constant ache they can't find a way to ease.

The tragedy happened.

How do we live from that day forward?

And THAT becomes OUR lesson.

When I lost my Daddy, it was to disease. I miss him, I think of him often. I remember and cherish the memories of our life.

And I know now HE is at peace in a way he never was here.

When I lost my sister, Diane, it was to mental illness. I miss her to the depths of my soul. I think of her daily. I remember and cherish the memories of our lives as sisters. I would never wish her back to suffer again. I know SHE is at peace in a way she never was here.

When I lost my Bobby, it was to a disease. The loss was a physical pain that never really goes away. He is always in my heart. Always in my mind. I remember his wisdom, and the power of his insight. But he suffered an entire lifetime of things I would not wish on my worst enemy. I would never wish him back again to suffer in that way. I KNOW he is at peace in a way he never was here.

When I lost my Mother, it was to extreme age and dementia. But I lost MY mother many years before. I loved her to the depths of me. But witnessing her become a captive within her own body taught me something I would never before believed possible. I would never wish her back in that way. I prayed nightly for HER release. It was the most loving thing I knew to do. And I KNOW she is at peace now, in a way she could no longer be here.

I share these very personal things from my life as an illustration of how I learned to accept what life kept handing me. And I learned that no matter how much I loved, it was not meant to change the path of someone else.

So I love now. And I remember. And I will not be held captive in that moment of time, when someone else took their last breath.

As long as I breathe, they still live in my memory.

As long as I breathe, each day is a celebration that they were part of my life.

As long as I breathe--

www.ingramcontent.com/pod-product-compliance
Lightning Source LLC
LaVergne TN
LVHW051633080426
835511LV00016B/2335